DRUG EDUCATION LIBRARY

CLUB DRUGS

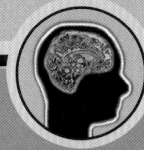

by Hal Marcovitz

LUCENT BOOKS

An imprint of Thomson Gale, a part of The Thomson Corporation

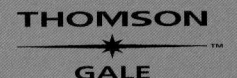

Detroit • New York • San Francisco • San Diego • New Haven, Conn.
Waterville, Maine • London • Munich

THOMSON

™

GALE

Produced by OTTN Publishing, Stockton, N.J.

© 2006 Thomson Gale, a part of The Thomson Corporation.

Thomson and Star Logo are trademarks and Gale and Lucent Books are registered trademarks used herein under license.

For more information, contact
Lucent Books
27500 Drake Rd.
Farmington Hills, MI 48331-3535
Or you can visit our Internet site at http://www.gale.com

LIBRARY OF CONGRESS CATALOGING-IN-PUBLICATION DATA

Marcovitz, Hal.
  Club drugs / by Hal Marcovitz.
    p. cm. — (Drug education library)
  Includes bibliographical references and index.
  ISBN 1-59018-517-X (hard cover : alk. paper) 1. Ecstasy
(Drug)—Juvenile literature. 2. Designer drugs—Juvenile literature.
3. Rave culture—Juvenile literature. 4. Drug abuse—Juvenile
literature. I. Title. II. Series.
  HV5822.M38M37 2006
  362.29'9—dc22
                        2005029472

Printed in the United States of America

CONTENTS

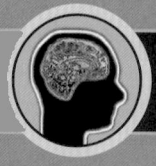

Foreword

The development of drugs and drug use in America is a cultural paradox. On the one hand, strong, potentially dangerous drugs provide people with relief from numerous physical and psychological ailments. Sedatives like Valium counter the effects of anxiety; steroids treat severe burns, anemia, and some forms of cancer; morphine provides quick pain relief. On the other hand, many drugs (sedatives, steroids, and morphine among them) are consistently misused or abused. Millions of Americans struggle each year with drug addictions that overpower their ability to think and act rationally. Researchers often link drug abuse to criminal activity, traffic accidents, domestic violence, and suicide.

These harmful effects seem obvious today. Newspaper articles, medical papers, and scientific studies have highlighted the myriad problems drugs and drug use can cause. Yet, there was a time when many of the drugs now known to be harmful were actually believed to be beneficial. Cocaine, for example, was once hailed as a great cure, used to treat everything from nausea and weakness to colds and asthma. Developed in Europe during the 1880s, cocaine spread quickly to the United States where manufacturers made it the primary ingredient in such everyday substances as cough medicines, lozenges, and tonics. Likewise, heroin, an opium derivative, became a popular painkiller during the late nineteenth century. Doctors and patients flocked to American drugstores to buy heroin, described as the optimal cure for even the worst coughs and chest pains.

As more people began using these drugs, though, doctors, legislators, and the public at large began to realize that they were more damaging than beneficial. After years of using heroin as a painkiller, for example, patients began asking their doctors for larger and stronger doses. Cocaine users reported dangerous side effects, including hallucinations and wild mood shifts. As a result, the U.S. government initiated more stringent regulation of many powerful and addictive drugs, and in some cases outlawed them entirely.

A drug's legal status is not always indicative of how dangerous it is, however. Some drugs known to have harmful effects can be purchased legally in the United States and elsewhere. Nicotine, a key ingredient in cigarettes, is known to be highly addictive. In an effort to meet their bodies' demands for nicotine, smokers expose themselves to lung cancer, emphysema, and other life-threatening conditions. Despite these risks, nicotine is legal almost everywhere.

Other drugs that cannot be purchased or sold legally are the subject of much debate regarding their effects on physical and mental health. Marijuana, sometimes described as a gateway drug that leads users to other drugs, cannot legally be used, grown, or sold in this country. However, some research suggests that marijuana is neither addictive nor a gateway drug and that it might actually benefit cancer and AIDS patients by reducing pain and encouraging failing appetites. Despite these findings and occasional legislative attempts to change the drug's status, marijuana remains illegal.

The Drug Education Library examines the paradox of drugs and drug use in America by focusing on some of the most commonly used and abused drugs or categories of drugs available today. By discussing objectively the many types of drugs, their intended purposes, their effects (both planned and unplanned), and the controversies surrounding them, the books in this series provide readers with an understanding of the complex role drugs and drug use play in American society. Informative sidebars, annotated bibliographies, and organizations to contact lists highlight the text and provide young readers with many opportunities for further discussion and research.

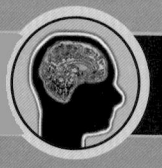
A New Drug Threat

Since the 1990s, growing numbers of young people have discovered a new class of drugs. Substances in this category became known as "club drugs" because at first, the drugs typically were consumed at parties, nightclubs, and large dance events known as raves. In recent years, though, use of club drugs has spread beyond the rave scene. Club drugs, like other illegal substances, are both sold on urban street corners and consumed by middle-class young people in comfortable suburban neighborhoods.

What Are Club Drugs?

Four substances are generally regarded as club drugs: 3,4-methylenedioxymethamphetamine (also known as MDMA or, most commonly, ecstasy); ketamine, a drug intended to be used as an animal tranquilizer; and Rohypnol and gamma-hydroxybutyrate (GHB), two drugs that are often employed in date-rape assaults.

Club drug use exploded among young people during the 1990s, but according to the University of Michigan's annual *Monitoring the Future* study—which charts drug use by

eighth, tenth, and twelfth grade students—use of these substances has declined in recent years. For example, the *Monitoring the Future* study reported that in 2001, more than 9 percent of all high school seniors reported that they had consumed ecstasy during the previous year. By 2004, that number had fallen to 4 percent. Lloyd Johnston, principal investigator for the *Monitoring the Future* study, explained, "Because ecstasy use had been in a pattern of sharp increase in recent years, its turnaround . . . and continued decline in all three grades . . . were very important developments."[1]

PERCENTAGE OF STUDENTS USING CLUB DRUGS, 2000–2004

Past Year Use of MDMA (Ecstasy)

Grade Level	2000	2001	2002	2003	2004
8th Grade	3.1%	3.5%	2.9%	2.1%	1.7%
10th Grade	5.4%	6.2%	4.9%	3.0%	2.4%
12th Grade	8.2%	9.2%	7.4%	4.5%	4.0%

Past Year Use of GHB

Grade Level	2000	2001	2002	2003	2004
8th Grade	2.1%	1.1%	0.8%	0.9%	0.7%
10th Grade	1.1%	1.0%	1.4%	1.4%	0.8%
12th Grade	1.9%	1.6%	1.5%	1.4%	2.0%

Past Year Use of Ketamine

Grade Level	2000	2001	2002	2003	2004
8th Grade	1.6%	1.3%	1.3%	1.1%	0.9%
10th Grade	2.1%	2.1%	2.2%	1.9%	1.3%
12th Grade	2.5%	2.5%	2.6%	2.1%	1.9%

Past Year Use of Rohypnol

Grade Level	2000	2001	2002	2003	2004
8th Grade	0.5%	0.7%	0.3%	0.5%	0.6%
10th Grade	0.8%	1.0%	0.7%	0.6%	0.7%
12th Grade	0.8%	0.9%	1.6%	1.3%	1.6%

Ecstasy

("X", XTC, Adam, MDMA,)
(3-4 Methylenedioxymethamphetamin

Stimulant and Hallucinogenic properties

Effects up to 6 hours

- Physical Effect:
  - Dehydration
  - Increased body temperature
  - Increased blood pressure
  - Probable brain damage

High school students watch a presentation on how club drugs affect the human body.

Still, Johnston noted that while use of MDMA has fallen, the decline recorded in 2004 was not as sharp as the declines reported in previous years. In other words, while progress has been made toward stopping the drug's use, that progress has slowed. There are still many people willing to use ecstasy, as well as the other club drugs, despite the overwhelming scientific evidence that shows they are responsible for dramatic and devastating long-term physical and psychological effects.

Safe or Dangerous?

For years, proponents of ecstasy have touted MDMA as a "safe" drug. They suggest that the drug is not addictive and that its effects wear off quite rapidly. Even today, some mental health professionals believe the drug may have value for treating certain mental illnesses, and they have convinced the U.S. Food and Drug Administration (FDA) to authorize limited testing on people who suffer from depression. Although the FDA approved human trials in 2005, the agency limited the testing program to patients afflicted with severe cancers who have little chance of surviving their diseases. Those patients could not possibly be harmed by the long-term effects of the drug on their brains or bodies. If this program shows that ecstasy can lift the intense depression experienced by these cancer patients, additional tests may be warranted. Still, it will take many years of careful study to determine whether MDMA is, under certain circumstances, a beneficial drug and whether it can be safely prescribed to people who suffer from depression or other ailments.

Most medical professionals, educators, law enforcement officers, and social workers agree that MDMA and the other club drugs are harmful. People have died as a result of using each of these drugs, and they are known to cause a host of physical and psychological problems.

The date-rape drugs Rohypnol and GHB are particularly dangerous. Because both drugs have no taste or odor, a dose can easily be slipped into a soft drink or alcoholic beverage

and go undetected. Both drugs act quickly: A woman who unknowingly consumes one of these drugs is soon overcome, causing her to black out. Women who are assaulted while under the influence of these drugs often have little or no memory of what happened. In some cases, a victim may not even realize she has been sexually assaulted. As a result, many date-rape victims do not go to the hospital until it is too late for physical evidence to be obtained from their bodies. This means it is often difficult to prosecute date-rape cases.

Testifying in 2000 before a U.S. Senate panel investigating international narcotics control efforts, Alan I. Leshner, a former director of the National Institute on Drug Abuse (NIDA), warned, "The bottom line on club drugs, particularly MDMA, is that given our current knowledge about these drugs, they appear to be extremely risky for anyone's health." The NIDA is one group working to get more information on club drugs and to get that information disseminated. "The citizens of this nation," Leshner said, "deserve to know what the science is revealing about these drugs."[2]

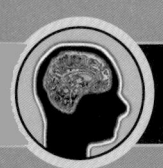

Chapter 1

RAVE CULTURE AND CLUB DRUGS

M usic and drug abuse have a long association in the United States. Throughout the twentieth century, some of America's most brilliant musicians—from Ray Charles to Kurt Cobain—became addicted to drugs. Starting in the late 1980s, a new class of narcotics was linked to music: club drugs, which owe their growth to the music and popularity of the rave culture.

Inside the Raves

Raves were born during the 1980s in European cities, particularly London, as private, after-hours dance parties. The music played at raves has a fast-paced, electric dance beat. Skilled rave deejays can mix beats and rhythms and employ laser light shows to keep the dancers moving for hours. Eventually, the raves outgrew nightclubs, and parties were staged in vacant warehouses and even remote open fields, sometimes drawing thousands of participants, including many teenagers. At first, news of rave parties was spread by word of mouth, but eventually promoters became quite open about the events, announcing them by passing out colorful handbills

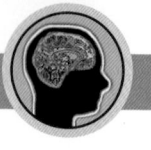

and posting notices in neighborhoods a few days before the parties. Soon, underground newspapers, slick magazines, and Internet pages were developed to publicize rave events. By the early 1990s, raves had arrived in the United States.

As rave culture spread, so did the use of the four club drugs. Certain characteristics of raves encouraged the use of these drugs. For instance, raves are long, sometimes lasting all night. Attendees dance virtually nonstop to fast, pulsating music (known as "house" or "techno" music), and it takes enormous energy for dancers to keep up. Ecstasy became popular at raves because it is a stimulant, which means it keeps its users awake, alert, and active. The drug also can cause hallucinations, which users say are enhanced by the loud, pounding music and the bright lights of the lasers. Also, the drug seems to heighten a user's senses, particularly the sense of touch. This seems to make dancing more pleasurable, and also provokes both simulated and actual sex acts in the dark corners of the rave venues. "The scenes within the

Laser beams show silhouettes of the dancers at a crowded rave. Raves typically feature pulsating lights and fast techno music.

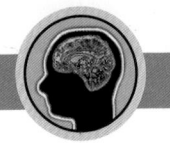

clubs were bizarre," Andrea Craparotta, a New Jersey investigator, told Congress in 2000. She described the scene:

> Unlike the thin, pale look of many heroin and crack cocaine users, Ecstasy users are primarily well-built, well-groomed, young adults. [They] would take Ecstasy and begin gyrating oddly to the pulsating 'techno' music. . . . patrons would constantly touch one another, regardless of gender. Sex acts were often simulated on the dance floor.[3]

Other observations are described in the book *Up All Night: A Closer Look at Club Drugs and Rave Culture*. Its author, psychotherapist Cynthia Knowles, warns:

> The rave experience is an uncontrolled clinical trial of the effects of club drugs on youth. A smorgasbord of drugs is offered for sale to a vulnerable and uneducated population of youth who take these new drugs in combination with other drugs or alcohol. There is danger in the product, danger in the dosing, and danger in the mixing. The long-term effects of the regular use of these drugs won't be known for at least a decade.[4]

Not Just in Big Cities

Once raves started attracting teenagers in urban locations, it did not take long for young people in suburban and rural areas to discover the new party culture as well. According to a 2001 U.S. Justice Department report,

> The increasing notoriety of raves has caused the rave culture to spread from major metropolitan areas to more rural or conservative locations. Rave parties are emerging in areas of Colorado, Iowa, Louisiana, Michigan, Minnesota, and Wisconsin that are not always prepared to manage unexpected crowds of teenagers."[5]

Instead of a lack of crowd preparation, however, it was a lack of knowledge about raves that initially made authorities

Although the first raves were held in nightclubs, the dance parties soon expanded into larger spaces like this warehouse.

ineffective in places like rural Brown County, South Dakota. In Brown County, parents were concerned when their teenagers started congregating at the local fairgrounds for late-night dance parties. They feared marijuana or alcohol was being abused at these parties. However, local police reported that there was no evidence either marijuana or alcohol were present at the weekly raves. In fact, the only thing police found unusual about the raves was the enormous volume of water the dancers seemed to consume. Most of the teens carried bottled water and drank steadily from their supplies. It took police a few months to figure out what was going on: Ecstasy causes its users to become extremely thirsty, and the dancers needed a constant source of water to quench their thirsts. Kim Dorsett, the deputy state's attorney who handles the county's juvenile crime cases, told *New York Times Upfront* magazine that the ecstasy use occurred "pretty much right under law enforcement's nose."[6]

Dorsett tried to spread a warning about ecstasy to young people in South Dakota. Traveling around the state, going from high school to high school, she could not help but no-

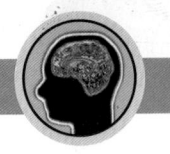

tice some telltale signs of ecstasy use. She found many students wearing necklaces strung with hard candy. Usually, she explained, there are ecstasy pills hidden among the mints hanging from such necklaces. "Our community really doesn't realize there's a problem yet," Dorsett told *New York Times Upfront.* "The teachers have no idea what they're looking at, and neither do the parents."[7]

Widespread Use

According to the U.S. Health and Human Services Department's Drug Abuse Warning Network (DAWN), which charts hospital emergency room visits by drug abusers, in 1994 hospital administrators in the United States reported just a handful of overdose cases involving ecstasy and GHB—a total of 250 throughout the entire country. Nearly a decade later,

Emergency Room Visits Related to MDMA (Ecstasy) Use, 1994–2002

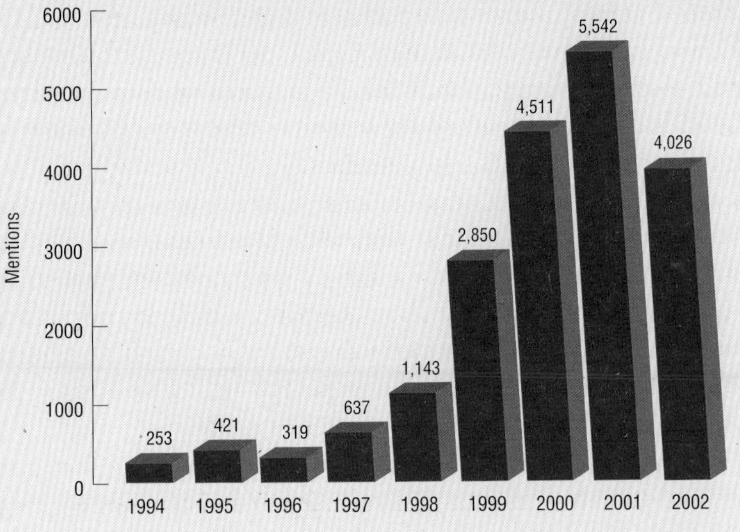

Source: Office of Applied Studies, SAMHSA, Drug Abuse Warning Network, 2005.

Mentions

Year	Mentions
1994	253
1995	421
1996	319
1997	637
1998	1,143
1999	2,850
2000	4,511
2001	5,542
2002	4,026

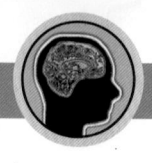
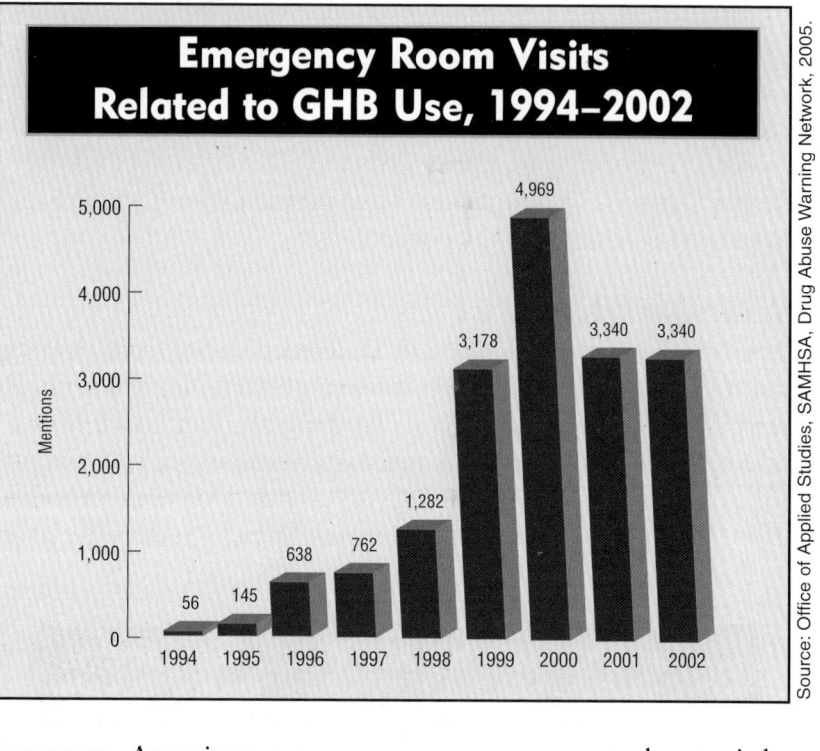

Emergency Room Visits Related to GHB Use, 1994–2002

Mentions

Year	Value
1994	56
1995	145
1996	638
1997	762
1998	1,282
1999	3,178
2000	4,969
2001	3,340
2002	3,340

however, American emergency rooms report about eight thousand ecstasy, ketamine, and GHB overdoses annually.

DAWN also has established that club drugs are primarily used by young people. In 2002, 75 percent of the club drug-related incidents reported by hospital emergency rooms involved patients age 26 and younger.

Law enforcement officials believe other drugs are also commonly used at raves; these include drugs such as LSD and methamphetamine. A 2003 DAWN report shows that in the early years of the twenty-first century, a new trend started making itself clear in emergency rooms: Club drug abusers were being treated for having ingested multiple drugs. According to a U.S. Justice Department report,

MDMA is unquestionably the most popular of the club drugs, and evidence of MDMA use by teenagers can be seen at most rave par-

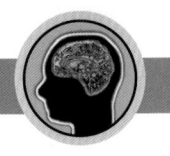

ties. Ketamine and GHB also are used at raves, as is Rohypnol, although to a lesser extent. A recent resurgence in the availability and use of some hallucinogens—LSD, PCP (phencyclidine), psilocybin, and peyote or mescaline—has also been noted at raves and dance clubs. . . . Inhalants like nitrous oxide are sometimes found at rave events; nitrous oxide is sold in gas-filled balloons called "whippets" for $5-$10.[8]

Usual Practices

Across the country, authorities have recorded common rave practices. Many ravers, for instance, wear rubber pacifiers—which are intended for babies—on strings around their necks. This is because ecstasy can cause bruxism, which is a tension of the jaws that can cause teeth to grind. The pacifiers help prevent bleeding gums and damage to users' teeth. Athletic

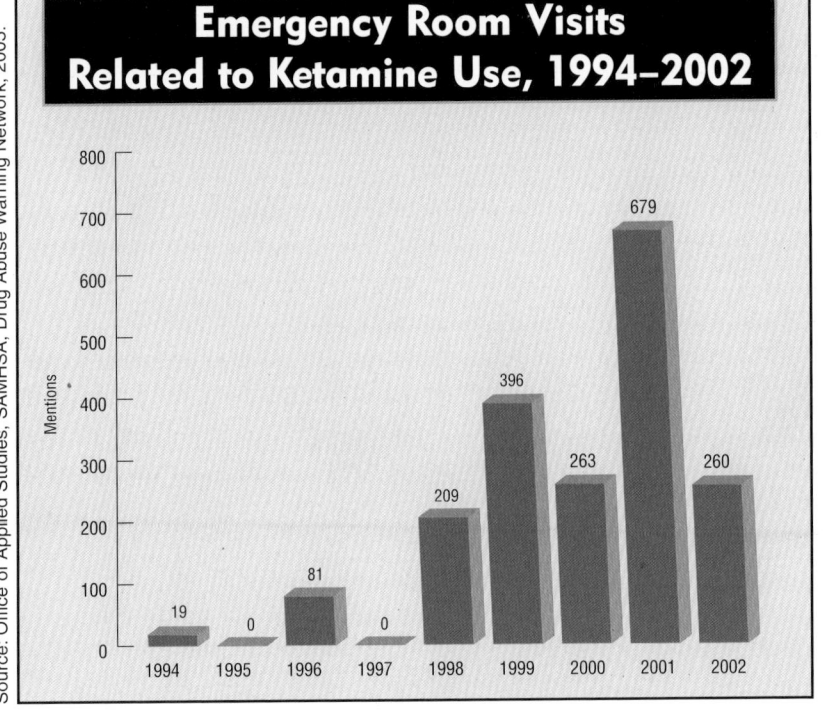

Source: Office of Applied Studies, SAMHSA, Drug Abuse Warning Network, 2005.

Emergency Room Visits Related to Ketamine Use, 1994–2002

Mentions

Year	Value
1994	19
1995	0
1996	81
1997	0
1998	209
1999	396
2000	263
2001	679
2002	260

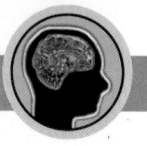

mouth guards—used by boxers and football players—may be used instead of pacifiers. Some ravers chew gum constantly or eat chewy candy like Tootsie Rolls to ease the tension on their jaws.

Another use for Tootsie Rolls is to conceal the ecstasy tablet itself. Dealers are known to sell the pills hidden inside the soft chocolate candy. Sometimes, taking ecstasy is known as "doing rolls," a reference to Tootsie Rolls.

Ecstasy users often carry jars of Vicks VapoRub—the product used by cold and flu sufferers to relieve congestion in their chests. The ingredients of VapoRub include menthol and eucalyptus, substances that intensify the MDMA high. Ecstasy users sometimes smear VapoRub on the inside of dust masks—the type worn by woodworkers—and wear them after swallowing a tablet of ecstasy to enhance their experience.

This raver is chewing on an infant pacifier. This is a indicator of ecstasy use, as the drug causes some users to grind their teeth.

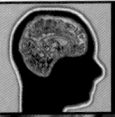 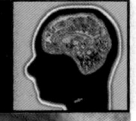

Many rave promoters sell what are known as "go-go drinks" at their events. Go-go drinks often contain extracts of the plants ginseng, yohimbine, and guarana, all of which are natural stimulants. (Guarana, for example, contains caffeine.) Go-go drinks help keep the dancers active during long periods of aerobic activity.

However, many doctors caution against using these natural products. Yohimbine can cause a rapid heartbeat, high blood pressure, and sleep disturbance. Go-go drinks are also believed to cause loss of appetite, nausea, visual impairment, and difficult or painful urination.

Other popular items worn by ravers are glow sticks—the kind usually sold to young children at Fourth of July fireworks events and similar celebrations. Ravers sometimes wear glow sticks in loops around their necks to enhance the drug's hallucinatory effects.

As use of club drugs became more widespread at raves, many promoters found ways to enhance the drug-taking experiences of the dancers. Because ecstasy is known to cause dehydration, which can be aggravated by the steamy club atmosphere as well as the intense physical exertion of dancing, bottled water is usually offered for sale at raves, although often at exorbitant prices. Some promoters also provide "chill rooms"—quiet places where dancers can settle down and come off their ecstasy highs. Additionally, it is not unusual for dancers to find T-shirts and other clothes that glorify ecstasy use for sale at the rave venues. A butterfly is recognized as the international symbol of ecstasy use, so clothes worn by ravers often display butterflies or simply the emblems "E" or "X," which are common abbreviations for the drug.

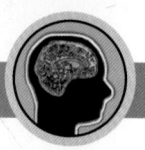

Tweaking the Frequencies

Ecstasy use is common at raves is because of its effect on the user's enjoyment of music and dancing. Simon Reynolds, author of the book *Generation Ecstasy*, found that the producers and deejays pick music and play it in ways designed to feed into the dancers' MDMA highs. A skilled deejay, he reports,

[can] tweak the frequencies, harmonics, and stereo imaging of different sounds, making them leap out of the mix with an eerie three-dimensionality or glisten with a hallucinatory vividness. Today's house track is a forever-fluctuating, fractal mosaic of glow-pulses and flicker-riffs, a teasing tapestry whose different strands take turns to move in and out of the sonic spotlight. Experienced under the influence of MDMA, the effect is . . . like tremulous fingertips tantalizing the back of your neck, or the simultaneously aural/tactile equivalent of a shimmer. In a sense, Ecstasy turns the entire body surface into an ear, an ultrasensitized membrane that responds to certain frequencies.[9]

The best deejays know how to connect with the dancers. In fact, ravers consider deejays to be true artists—even though they did not write the music or record it, their skill in remixing the music and enhancing it to please the crowd is a much-valued talent.

Another reason ravers take MDMA is because it stimulates a portion of the brain that encourages the user to perform the same activities over and over again, never tiring of the repetitiveness—seemingly perfect for all-night rave dancing. According to Reynolds:

The music's emphasis on texture and timbre enhances the drug's mildly synthetic effects so that sounds seem to caress the listener's skin. You feel like you're dancing inside the music; sound becomes a fluid medium in which you're immersed. . . . Rave music's hypnotic beats and sequenced loops also make it perfectly suited to

Rave deejays often play music intended to enhance the high produced by ecstasy or other drugs.

interact with another attribute of Ecstasy: recent research suggests the drug . . . encourages repetitive behavior.[10]

Society's Equalizer

In American society, people are expected to be productive and successful in their jobs or at school. Each day, many people endure what they perceive as the petty jealousies and prejudices of others. But dancers often share a belief that raves are society's greatest equalizer—no one is rich or poor at a rave, and no one is a better athlete, better student, or even a better dancer.

Reynolds believes ecstasy has a lot to do with drawing ravers into a common mindset and making them feel as though they are part of one common, pulsating organism on the dance floor. He explains that the drug helps induce a feeling of attachment to others. "When large numbers of people took Ecstasy together, the drug catalyzed a strange and wondrous atmosphere of collective intimacy, an electric sense of

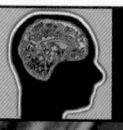 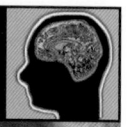

A troubling trend that has recently been identified is that use of drugs like LSD and methamphetamine have become more common at raves and among users of club drugs. A raver may take a dose of ecstasy to enhance the music and the rave environment, then a dose of another drug to achieve a far-different type of high. This is known as "stacking" or "cocktailing." "Candyflipping" is another term ravers use, which means mixing the drugs MDMA and LSD. Similarly, "kittyflipping" refers to mixing ecstasy with ketamine.

However, combining two or more drugs can have fatal consequences. "Stacking increases the risk of overdose, as the stimulant effects of MDMA may mask the sedative effects of alcohol or opiates," Ellen S. Rome, the head of adolescent medicine at the Cleveland Clinic, warned in the *Cleveland Clinic Journal of Medicine*.

Using alcohol with MDMA (known as "boosting") can be particularly dangerous. Ecstasy causes dehydration, while alcohol often acts as a diuretic, meaning it encourages urination. Mixing alcohol and MDMA prompts the body to rid itself of fluids at an enormously accelerated pace.

LSD is sometimes used in conjunction with club drugs.

Ellen S. Rome, "It's a Rave New World: Rave Culture and Illicit Drug Use in the Young," *Cleveland Clinic Journal of Medicine*, June 2001, p. 544.

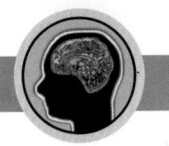

connection between complete strangers,"[11] Reynolds wrote in *Generation Ecstasy.*

In a *Time* magazine article, a raver named Adrienne explained how the drug made her feel:

> I had always been aloof or insecure or snobby, however you want to put it. And I took [ecstasy] and realized, you know what, we're all here; we're all dancing; we're not so different. I allowed myself to get closer to people.[12]

One unfortunate consequence of rave culture is that many young people have mistakenly come to believe that ecstasy use is mandatory at a rave. In fact, use of ecstasy at raves is so widespread that one group of researchers found nearly all the dancers they approached at rave events reported using ecstasy at some point in their lives. The researchers' study was conducted by the Pacific Institute for Research and Evaluation, a Maryland-based group that assesses public policy issues.

These researchers interviewed seventy dancers at raves during April and May 2002. At each rave, the interviews were conducted between midnight and 5 A.M. Eighty-five percent of the dancers that the interviewers approached agreed to answer questions. In fact, the dancers did not hesitate to admit having taken club drugs and other types of drugs—even though taking them is illegal. After conducting the interviews, the Pacific Institute's researchers recounted, "Eighty-six percent of the respondents reported lifetime ecstasy use [having used the drug at some point in their lives], 51 percent reported 30-day use, and 30 percent reported using ecstasy within the two days preceding the interview."[13]

Unconcerned About the Danger

Studies indicate that people who do not use club drugs have a clearer understanding of their dangers. According to the Pacific Institute researchers, "non-ecstasy users were significantly more likely than past-year users to perceive risks associated with the regular use of alcohol and ecstasy. Not

23

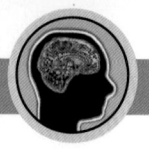

surprisingly, non-ecstasy users were significantly more likely than past-year users to perceive harmful long-term physical and psychological effects associated with ecstasy ingestion."[14]

Others have reported on both the widespread use of ecstasy and the lack of concern by users about its dangers. For example, in his book *Rave Culture: An Insider's Overview*, author Jimi Fritz interviewed many ravers who downplayed the dangers of club drugs, emphasizing their positive experiences. Seattle rave deejay Troy Roberts told Fritz, "I tried ecstasy for the first time on Halloween. I was dancing to a tribal house mix of k.d. lang's 'Lifted by Love' and it sounded like a voice coming down from heaven. I was smiling from one side of my face to the other and remember screaming for about four hours."[15] A Canadian raver, who identified himself to Fritz as "J," told the author:

> Ecstasy took me back to a place where I was before adolescence. When the world seemed new and I wasn't limited by my immediate past. It made me think about what I wanted to do and what was important in life. It reminded me of when I was a child and didn't feel guilty or ashamed or anxious about anything.[16]

Fritz spoke to many such rave fans who did not acknowledge ecstasy's harms.

Intended for Legitimate Uses

Club drugs did not become widely abused substances until relatively recently. Each of the club drugs were developed decades ago, and in some cases are still used for legitimate medical purposes. But in the United States, with few exceptions, club drugs remain illegal substances that are available only through underground channels.

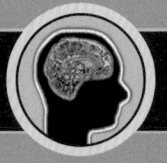

Chapter 2

THE EVOLUTION OF CLUB DRUGS

Each of the four club drugs was developed for scientific or medical purposes and, in fact, two of the drugs still have legitimate uses. Veterinarians in the United States sometimes use ketamine as a painkiller for their animal patients. Rohypnol is illegal in the United States but legal in some seventy countries in South America, Central America, and Europe; doctors find it to be an effective anesthetic in surgeries that require the patient to respond or otherwise cooperate during the procedures. However, ketamine, Rohypnol, and the other club drugs are widely abused in the United States.

Birth of Ecstasy

MDMA was first developed in 1912 at the German pharmaceutical company Merck. Researchers discovered the substance while searching for a drug that would stop bleeding. Although MDMA did not fit that need, some of the Merck researchers believed MDMA could become useful as an "intermediate" chemical, meaning that it could be employed in research on other drugs that Merck wished to develop.

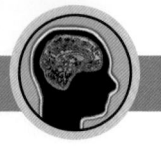
Ecstasy pills come in a variety
of shapes, sizes, and colors.

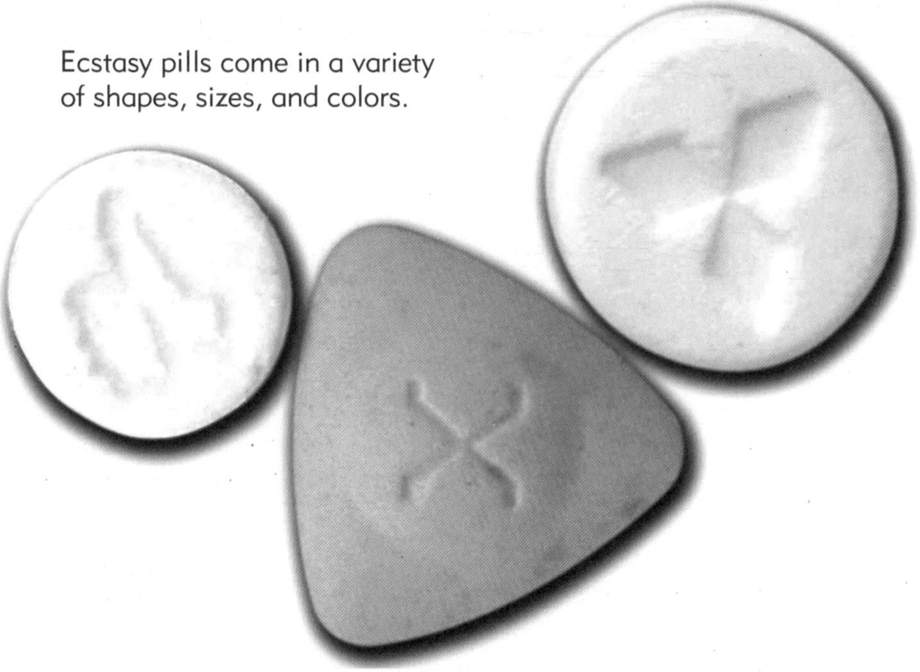

As its name suggests, 3,4-methylenedioxymethampheta-
mine is chemically similar to methamphetamine, which today
takes the form of the abused drugs known as speed or crystal
meth. MDMA also contains some of the same chemicals that
make up the drug mescaline, a hallucinogenic substance that
causes psychedelic "trips" similar to those caused by LSD.

Merck researchers never did find a legitimate use for
MDMA, and the drug disappeared for decades. MDMA did
not surface again until 1953 when, during the Cold War, the
U.S. Army tested a number of experimental drugs, including
MDMA, to determine whether they might be effective in ex-
tracting information from captured spies. In 1969, the U.S.
Army declassified the results of its drug tests. According to
the army's documents, MDMA was one of eight drugs administered during testing under an army contract with the
University of Michigan. The drug was given to rats, mice,
guinea pigs, dogs, and monkeys. Another drug administered
to animals during the tests was a derivative of MDMA—

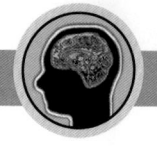

methylenedioxamphetamine, or MDA. In the military test, no humans were given MDMA or MDA, but during a separate program at the New York Psychiatric Institute, a large dose of MDA was inadvertently given to a human subject who subsequently died.

MDA found its way into the illegal drug culture before MDMA did, arriving on the streets of the Haight-Ashbury district of San Francisco during the 1960s. At the time, there was an abundance of other, better-known drugs in Haight-Ashbury, including marijuana, LSD, and speed, but MDA soon developed a loyal following. It came to be known as the "love drug" or the "mellow drug" because it enhanced feelings of empathy (the ability to identify with another person's feelings) and great joy, which lasted for six or eight hours. (MDMA has also been called the love drug by some users.)

In 1970, biochemist Alexander Shulgin started a series of experiments with MDMA that included tests on human subjects, including himself and his wife Ann. In 1978, Shulgin published the results of his MDMA tests, finding that the drug created "an easily controlled altered state of consciousness with emotional and sensual overtones."[17] Later, Shulgin also declared the drug "could be all things to all people."[18] He suggested MDMA could be put to a number of uses, such as helping people emerge from depression, curing speech impediments, and serving as a recreational substance. By the early 1980s, psychiatrists were prescribing it to their patients to prompt them to talk about their feelings during therapy.

Quick Popularity

Around this time the underground drug culture discovered MDMA. The drug quickly became popular in the Southwest. Drug dealers in Texas sold it in small brown bottles, calling it "Sassyfras," evidently because Merck chemists had used sassafras oil in the original synthesis of the drug. At that time, MDMA was not illegal, so it was sold openly at nightclubs and bars in the Dallas and Fort Worth areas. People could

Dr. Alexander Shulgin, the man responsible for much of the research on MDMA, conducts an experiment in his Berkeley, California, lab.

even buy it by calling a toll-free telephone number. During the early 1980s, it was estimated that some 30,000 tablets a month were sold in Texas.

Senator Lloyd Bentsen of Texas soon demanded that the U.S. Drug Enforcement Administration (DEA) investigate whether this popular drug was safe. When federal officials began examining the drug sales, MDMA manufacturers stepped up production, anticipating that their operations might get shut down. In 1985, the DEA reported that use of MDMA was widespread in twenty-eight states and that research indicated the drug caused brain damage in lab rats. As a result of these findings, on July 1, 1985, the federal government declared MDMA an illegal substance.

During the mid-1980s, the drug began appearing at raves and parties in Europe. It is believed the drug first became popular in the club culture on the Mediterranean island of

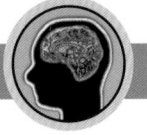

Ibiza near Spain. From there, young British tourists who had been vacationing on the island and had discovered MDMA took it to England, where it became popular in London's clubs. A short time later, MDMA crossed the ocean and began to appear at American nightclubs and raves.

In the United States, MDMA was known first as "Adam" and then as "ecstasy." The drug dealer who thought up the

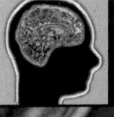 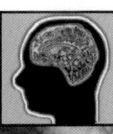

Shulgin: Ecstasy Can Be Safe

Nearly three decades after he promoted the use of MDMA to treat mental illness, Alexander Shulgin still believes the drug was unfairly banned by the federal government. In his view, the government overreacted to the drug's widespread use at raves. In an interview with Julie Holland, Shulgin said:

Am I happy about where MDMA stands now? No, I am quite sad. Here is a compound, an incredibly safe compound when used appropriately, that has the potential of giving pleasure to the user and of being of medical value to those who have certain psychological problems. . . . And yet, for political and self-serving reasons, the authorities have demonized it and made it a felony to possess and use. In effect, they forbid information about its virtues to be made available. I am proud to have had some hand in uncovering its value, but I am sad to see it become illegal and thus effectively unavailable to those who could benefit from it.

Quoted in Julie Holland, ed., *Ecstasy: The Complete Guide*. Rochester, VT: Park Street Press, 2001, p. 12.

29

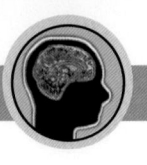
name *ecstasy* admitted that he wanted to make the drug sound sexy, even though the sense of closeness that the drug produced would be described more accurately by another term. "Empathy would be more appropriate," he said, "but how many people know what it means?"[19]

The Origins of Ketamine

Decades after MDMA was first produced, during the 1950s, scientists at the Detroit-based drug manufacturer Parke-Davis were searching for an effective anesthesia that would put patients to sleep and dull their pain. In 1956, they developed a drug that seemed to fill both needs: phencyclidine, which became commonly known as PCP.

At first, PCP was regarded as a miracle drug—it was found to be an effective surgical painkiller in very low doses. But soon the side effects of PCP became evident. The drug caused its users to dissociate, meaning they entered deep hallucinations in which they lost touch with reality. Phencyclidine often was found to send its users into uncontrollable and violent rages. The dangers of these rages were compounded by the fact that, because PCP is a painkiller, users do not feel pain when they punch their fists through windows or otherwise injure themselves. Therefore, pain does not cut short the rages, and injured users do not always realize the need for medical attention.

PCP was quickly shelved, but Parke-Davis still hoped to find a safer derivative of phencyclidine that would not cause hallucinations or violent outbursts. A breakthrough seemed to have occurred in 1962, when Wayne State University biochemist Calvin Stevens, working in a research program sponsored by Parke-Davis, developed the drug ketamine hydrochloride, which he labeled "CI-1581." In 1965, Parke-Davis began testing the new drug on humans. Edward F. Domino, the pharmacology professor at the medical school of the University of Michigan who headed the testing program, wrote:

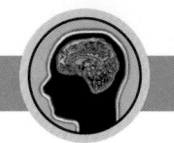

.None of us shall ever forget the amazing spectrum of clinical pharmacological effects that this agent produced in the volunteers we studied. So unique were these effects that we had to invent a new set of words to describe its anesthetic properties. The drug produced "zombies" who were totally disconnected from their environment, with their eyes open, and yet in a complete anesthetic and analgesic state. The observation of being disconnected from the environment gave rise to the term "dissociative anesthesia."[20]

Domino and his colleagues believed that the drug now known as ketamine could be "a unique and safe anesthetic agent," although Domino noted that the drug's users hallucinated. The researchers recommended that ketamine be administered in very small doses under the strict control of medical professionals. "Since ketamine has some actions clearly related to phencyclidine," Domino explained, "we have tried to find ways to reduce the 'bad effects' of ketamine—or to 'tame the tiger.'"[21]

Ketamine was initially developed as a painkiller. The drug is still used for that purpose by some veterinarians.

Ketamine can be found as a powder as well as a liquid. Here, a young man cuts lines of powder ketamine during a party.

Parke-Davis received a patent for ketamine in 1966, and in 1970 the U.S. Food and Drug Administration granted permission for the drug to be used as an anesthetic in both humans and animals. Parke-Davis marketed the drug under the names "Ketalar" and "Ketaject." One of the first places the new drug was employed was on the battlefields of Vietnam, where it was administered to wounded soldiers. It was felt that under the small doses recommended by Domino, the dissociative qualities of the drug could be controlled. That proved to be the case. However, as word spread about the drug's hallucinogenic features, it did not take long for ketamine to find its way into the hands of drug users, who took it in quantities large enough to promote hallucinations. The drug was sold illegally as pills; in powder form, so it could be snorted through the nose or sprinkled on tobacco or marijuana; and in liquid form, so that it could be mixed into drinks or injected intravenously.

Entrenched in the Underground

One of the first studies of the illegal use of ketamine was performed in the 1970s by Karl Jansen, a psychiatrist at Maudsley Hospital in London, England. Jansen spoke with a drug user who burglarized a veterinary office where he found "this stuff called Ketalar." After injecting the drug, Jansen wrote, the user found himself "floating somewhere above the roof."[22]

In 1978, two books describing firsthand accounts of ketamine use were published. The books—*Journeys into the Bright World* by Marcia Moore and *The Scientist* by John Lilly—described mind-bending experiences by the authors while they were under the influence of ketamine. Lilly, a physician, even claimed to have made contact with extraterrestrials while under the drug's influence. Describing his experiences on ketamine, Lilly wrote:

> I was a head on a flying carpet, flying through my mind, smiling.
> I was getting new Knowledge from K. K taught me so much in a
> very short period of time. It Knew everything. It said, "Every-
> thing ever Known is stored and can be visited." Also it said,
> "Knowledge starts with K for a reason." And many other tidbits
> of Knowledge. I asked it why I loved to trip so much, it said, "For
> the good of Man." Hmmm, I wasn't sure what that meant, but I
> Knew all along that it did have a purpose. K doesn't speak in audi-
> ble words, it is like Knowledge implanted as you need to Know it.
> If you have a question that you've never been able to figure out,
> K will put the answer in your mind so you Know it. It is strange
> that way. Once you Know it, nothing can shake that out of you.
> You really Know it.[23]

Ketamine quickly became an entrenched part of the illegal drug culture. Because of the danger of abuse, most physicians stopped prescribing the drug, although in recent years some doctors are again considering it as an analgesic for the most severe types of pain. In 1999, the drug became a federally controlled substance.

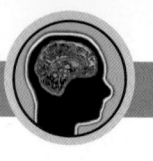

When used legally, ketamine is employed mostly by veterinarians, but even they use it only under certain conditions. Says Texas veterinarian Wayne Kyle, "There is no situation where a veterinarian will give Ketamine to a pet owner for home treatment of the animal. It is only used in surgery and under strict supervision of the veterinarian."[24]

Most ketamine that is used illegally is obtained from drug traffickers who steal it from veterinary offices or import it from Mexico, where it can be found in pharmacies. Unlike ecstasy or GHB, ketamine is rarely cooked in illegal basement labs because it is difficult to manufacture.

Rohypnol

Rohypnol, one of the other popular club drugs, is the trade name for flunitrazepam, a drug manufactured legally outside the United States by the Swiss drug maker Hoffman-LaRoche. The company introduced the drug in 1975 as an anesthetic and as a treatment for insomnia. Rohypnol is in the class of drugs known as benzodiazepines. These are depressants, or tranquilizers, meaning they slow the brain and body functions. Rohypnol's effects are similar to those of the widely prescribed tranquilizer Valium, but Rohypnol is considered ten times more potent. By the late 1970s, it had become a commonly abused drug in Europe.

In 1983, the DEA declared Rohypnol a controlled substance. However, because the drug had never been approved for sale in the United States, American doctors were not permitted to write prescriptions for it. And even if a patient could somehow convince a doctor to write a prescription, pharmacists could not fill them. In 1996, the Food and Drug Administration placed a further limitation on the drug, making it illegal to import Rohypnol into the United States.

Although Rohypnol possession was illegal, it began appearing in the country during the 1990s. It is believed the drug began to become widely available after the fall of 1992. Supposedly, Mexican laborers employed to fix the roofs on homes

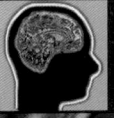 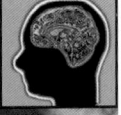

John Lilly, the physician who promoted the use of ketamine in his book *The Scientist*, said he learned about the drug after it was prescribed to him by another physician as a cure for his chronic headaches. When ketamine made his headaches go away, Lilly found himself curious about what else the drug could accomplish.

Lilly attempted to enhance the hallucinatory properties of the drug by immersing himself in what he called a sensory deprivation tank. Lilly filled a bath-sized tank with heavily salted warm water and wore a breathing mask so he could remain submerged in the tank for hours. Thus, he would be isolated from all sights, sounds, and smells around him. Before submerging, he consumed a dose of ketamine.

During the 1970s, Dr. John Lilly wrote about his experiments with ketamine.

Lilly's ketamine trips were usually intense, often bizarre, and sometimes dangerous. One time, according to *The Little Book of Ketamine*, while under the influence of ketamine Lilly attempted to call the White House to warn the president of "the intervention in human affairs of the solid-state life forms elsewhere in the galaxy." Still other times he was hospitalized, and once he was found unconscious and face down in his swimming pool.

Quoted in Kit Kelly, *The Little Book of Ketamine*. Berkeley, CA: Ronin Publishing, 1999, p. 20.

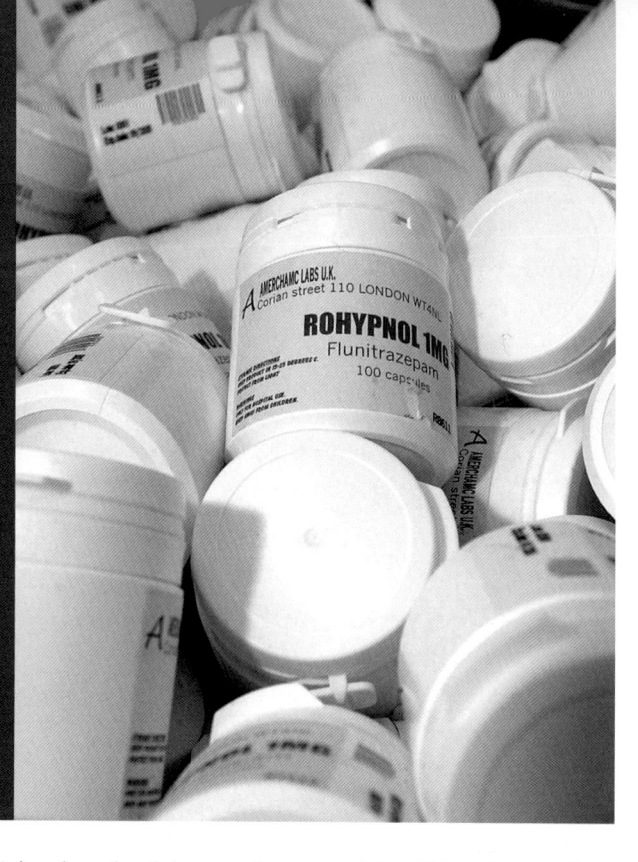

Although Rohypnol is illegal in the United States, it is legally available in Europe and other parts of the world.

in South Florida that had been damaged by Hurricane Andrew used the drug and sold it locally, giving Rohypnol its nickname—"roofies." Rohypnol is sold in tablets, although the pills can be crushed and snorted.

While Rohypnol is regarded as a club drug, it may be more accurate to describe it as a "frat drug," because in its early history in the United States it was found mostly at college fraternity parties. When Rohypnol is dissolved in liquid, it does not change the odor or taste of the drink, so it was often given to unsuspecting females. In 1996, Clark Staten, executive director of the Chicago-based Emergency Response and Research Institute, wrote:

> According to a University of Florida drug hotline, "Roofies" are often combined with alcohol, marijuana, or cocaine to produce a rapid and very dramatic "high." Even when used by itself, users can appear extremely intoxicated, with slurred speech, no coordination, swaying, and blood-shot eyes . . . with no odor of alcohol. The drug has been added to punch and other drinks at fraternity

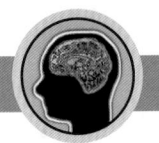

parties and college social gatherings, where it is reportedly given to female party participants in hopes of lowered inhibitions and facilitating sexual conquest. Police departments in several parts of the country say that after ingestion of "Roofies" that several young women have reported waking up in frat houses with no clothes on, finding themselves in unfamiliar surroundings with unfamiliar people, or having actually been sexually assaulted while under the influence of the drug.[25]

Goob

Similar to Rohypnol, and also used as a date rape drug, is gamma-hydroxybutyrate, or GHB. The development of GHB dates back to 1961, when it was synthesized as an anesthetic by French biochemist Henri Laborit. During experimentation on the drug, it actually was found to have few painkilling qualities. Instead, patients taking the substance experienced seizures—jerking movements of the legs, arms, and head. It was quickly determined that GHB would not be an effective anesthesia.

Before GHB was declared illegal in 1990, the substance was sold as a bodybuilding supplement in sports nutrition stores.

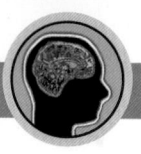

In the 1980s, bodybuilders discovered GHB. They saw it as beneficial in promoting the creation of muscle mass and causing weight gain. GHB was sold legally on the shelves of health food stores until authorities started learning of the drug's dangerous side effects. In 1990, the Food and Drug Administration banned sales of GHB in the United States. In 2000, in response to some sixty deaths reported from GHB use, the DEA declared GHB a controlled substance, making it a crime to possess the drug in the United States.

GHB, which is known on the street as "goob," has been found to produce tranquilizing effects much faster than Rohypnol. This is one reason it has been used as a date-rape drug. In small quantities, GHB is known to produce feelings of euphoria as well as hallucinations. This makes it a popular drug on the rave scene, where ravers seem unconcerned about or may be unaware of its dangerous side effects.

Irreversible Health Effects

There is a good reason that all four of the major club drugs are either banned outright or strictly regulated in the United States. All the drugs can cause both short- and long-term effects on the brain and body. Some of those effects are irreversible. In MDMA's case, for example, there is growing evidence suggesting the drug causes permanent brain damage, resulting in chronic memory loss in its users. There is also evidence that shows MDMA can lead to psychiatric illness—users report that they find themselves enduring long periods of depression after giving up ecstasy. Aside from such negative consequences, all four drugs also include the very real possibility that just a single dose can prove fatal.

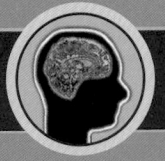

Chapter 3

The Physical Effects of Club Drugs

Each of the club drugs causes different effects. Rohypnol is a depressant, meaning it slows down the brain, central nervous system, and motor functions. GHB is a tranquilizer, but it is also known to produce euphoria and hallucinations. Ketamine is a dissociative hallucinogen; the drug causes its users to become unhinged from reality but without the tranquilizing effects of GHB or Rohypnol. MDMA is a stimulant, energizing its users. All four of these drugs have significant consequences for habitual users, causing both short-term and long-term damage to their brains and bodies.

Affecting Neurotransmitters

Club drugs are like most narcotics in that they alter the activity of neurotransmitters, chemicals in the brain that deliver messages from cell to cell. Nerve cells throughout the brain and body are known as neurons; each person has millions. Each neuron emits electrical impulses containing messages that control the body's functions. By passing these impulses through the body's network of nerve cells, the neurons work together to tell a foot to take a step, or a

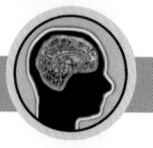

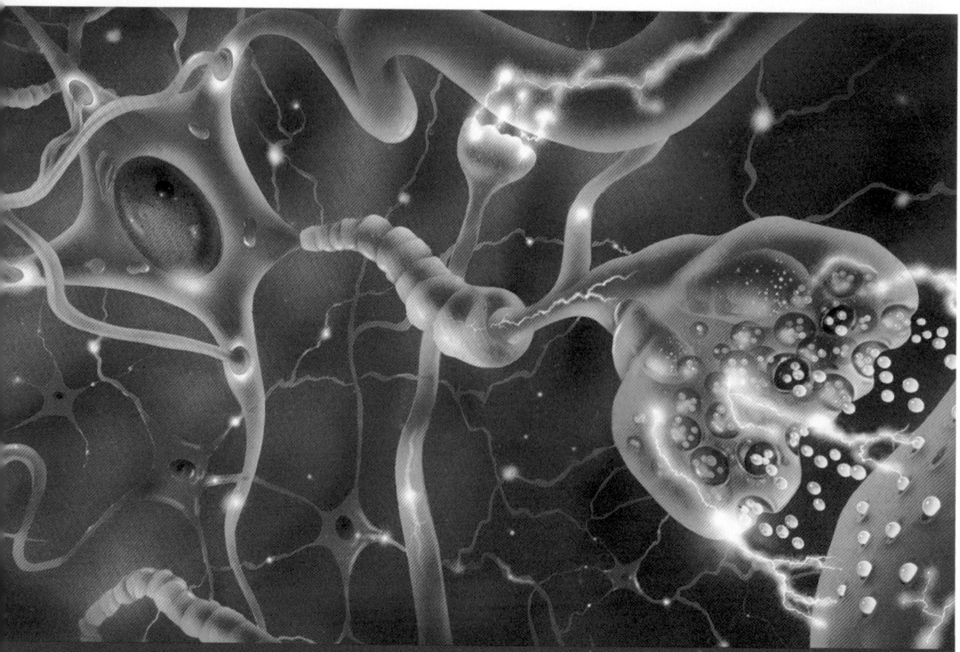

This illustration shows messages, or impulses, being sent between neurons in the brain. Club drugs affect these impulses by interfering with the release of neurotransmitters.

hand to hold a pencil, or the lips to form words so that the person may speak.

Impulses travel along large stems of neurons, known as axons, to smaller stems known as dendrites. When an impulse reaches the end of an axon, it will jump over a tiny space known as a synapse on its journey to the dendrite of the next neuron. To enable the electrical impulse to make the jump, the neuron releases a neurotransmitter to carry the message. On the end of each neuron's dendrite is a group of molecules known as receptors, which accept specific neurotransmitters and then transmit the impulse to the next synapse. Not all neurotransmitters carry messages, though; some neurotransmitters prevent unwanted messages from passing from neuron to neuron.

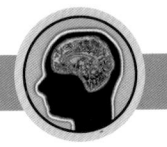

Drugs influence the transmission of information in the brain. The drug may produce a flood of neurotransmitters so that too many messages are delivered to the neurons. Or, it may neutralize the neurotransmitters that work to block unwanted information, causing a flood of unwanted messages to reach the neurons.

MDMA causes a rush of three neurotransmitters—serotonin, dopamine, and norepinephrine. Serotonin helps regulate mood, sleep, pain, emotion, and appetite. The excess amount of serotonin produced by MDMA causes an elevation in users' moods and is also believed to be responsible for causing hallucinations. "You might feel a big-time mood lift; an intense bond with anyone you happen to run into; a rush of energy; the urge to talk your head off; or happy hallucinations," wrote Larry Smith in an article about the drug. "Ecstasy triggers a big blast of the brain chemical serotonin, which puts you in a great mood in a hurry. Your inhibitions will disappear and you'll love everything around you, from music to people to plants."[26]

Deep Depression

Ecstasy also causes a surge in the neurotransmitter dopamine, which enables the body to move and also regulates emotions, particularly the feeling of pleasure. Over time, constant and regular surges of dopamine can lead to long-lasting effects. This is because when too much dopamine is released, the brain compensates by permanently reducing the number of dopamine receptors. Also, since the brain is responding to the stimulation of ecstasy to create dopamine, the body may make less dopamine on its own. Lack of dopamine contributes to depression. This means that a heavy ecstasy user may fall into periods of deep depression when he or she is not using the drug.

Because MDMA causes healthy, mentally stable users to fall into depression, what does it do to people who already suffer from depression? According to David M. McDowell, a

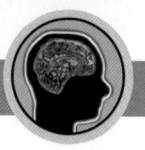

Columbia University psychology professor, the drug may push them even further into mental illness. In testimony before the U.S. House Judiciary Committee, McDowell said, "There are numerous case reports of a single dose of MDMA precipitating severe psychiatric illness. MDMA does induce a range of depressive symptoms and anxiety in some individuals, and for that reason, people with depression and anxiety should be specifically cautioned about the dangers of using MDMA."[27]

Finally, ecstasy causes a rush of norepinephrine, which enhances feelings of excitement, euphoria, and alertness in the user. As with the other neurotransmitters, norepinephrine's natural production by the body is scaled back during times when the user is not taking ecstasy, which therefore intensifies depression between doses. Norepinephrine also controls blood pressure and pulse rate, which explains why MDMA users may find their blood pressure and heartrate skyrocketing while under the influence of the drug.

Other Drugs' Effects on Neurotransmitters

Ketamine blocks the receptors that accept serotonin, dopamine, and norepinephrine as well as the neurotransmitter glutamate. Glutamate controls people's feelings of pain as well as memory and their perceptions of the environment. With the flow of glutamate interrupted, ketamine users can find themselves undergoing bizarre hallucinations—they lose touch with reality. Taking a ketamine trip is sometimes called "falling into the K hole."

Rohypnol affects the neurotransmitter gamma amino butyric acid (or GABA), causing it to bind to brain cells. When GABA binds to a brain cell, it slows down the cell's ability to function. Essentially, this makes people sleepy. In Europe, Rohypnol is sometimes prescribed as a cure for insomnia.

GHB may also affect GABA, causing it to bind to brain cells. In addition, GHB causes a serotonin rush, which elevates the mood of the user and may prompt hallucinations. GHB affects the neurotransmitter acetylcholine as well.

Depression is a common side effect of MDMA use. The drug can make existing problems with depression worse.

Acetylcholine regulates alertness. The release of too much acetylcholine can cause users to lose control of their muscles and even cause them to black out.

The flow of dopamine through the brain is also affected by GHB. Studies have shown the drug both enhances and inhibits this neurotransmitter, which means it can provide the users with either a rush of euphoria or an attack of anxiety.

By consuming ketamine, GHB, and Rohypnol, the user could fall into a deeply relaxed state, both physically and mentally. That is what makes the drugs so dangerous to date-rape victims—they lose the will to resist or even to know what is going on around them.

Dangerous Side Effects

All the club drugs produce short- and long-term side effects on users' brains and bodies. Some of those side effects can be devastating, and in many cases they are irreversible. The short-term side effects of Rohypnol, for example, include decreased blood pressure, memory impairment, drowsiness, visual disturbances, dizziness, confusion, upset stomach, and

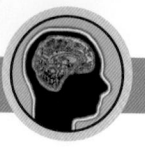

inability to urinate. Side effects of ketamine use can include difficulty breathing and an irregular heartbeat. GHB users may experience drowsiness, nausea, unconsciousness, and difficulty breathing. MDMA's side effects include lethargy, anorexia, decreased motivation, sleepiness, depression, fatigue, confusion, soaring body temperature, convulsions, racing heartbeat, and kidney failure. Although ecstasy is known as the "love drug," users report that while the drug enhances the sense of touch and makes them want to be close to others, it also reduces their ability to complete the sexual act.

Ecstasy may be at its most dangerous at raves, where it is consumed in the electric environment of the dance floor. Yet because the drug's effects are not compatible with solitude, few ecstasy users are known to take the drug at home or alone. "Ecstasy is above all a social drug," wrote *Generation Ecstasy* author Simon Reynolds. "It's rarely used by a solitary individual, because the feelings it unleashes would have nowhere to go. (A friend of mine, bored, once took some

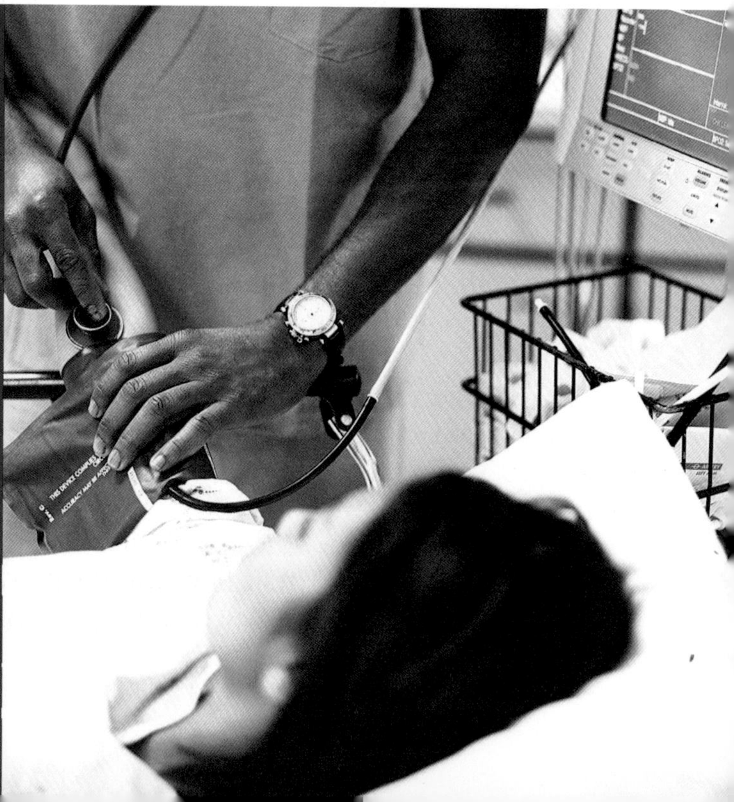

Club drugs can cause the user's heart rate and blood pressure to drop precipitously or rise rapidly.

leftover E at home and spent the night kissing the walls and hugging himself.)"[28]

On the other hand, one of the drug's effects on the body make it more dangerous when taken at a rave. The drug dehydrates its user and causes body temperature to rise. When a hot, steamy nightclub and all-night aerobic activity are added to the mix, the MDMA user risks heatstroke—a condition in which the body's temperature rises several degrees above normal. Heatstroke can cause permanent damage to the brain, heart, and other organs. In the book *Ecstasy: The Complete Guide*, Emanuel Sferios, the founder of DanceSafe, a group that promotes ecstasy education at raves, commented:

> At raves, the dance floor may be extremely hot, the promoters may overcrowd their venues . . . and the user may be dancing for many hours without replenishing lost body fluids. So when you're in a hot environment, engaging in intense aerobic activity, not replenishing your body fluids, and taking a stimulant-type drug that can inhibit your thermoregulatory ability [the body's natural temperature regulation], you can get heatstroke. In fact, you can remove the drug from the equation and still have heatstroke. We have seen people collapse on the dance floor from heatstroke when they haven't taken any drug.[29]

Addictive Properties

Another danger of club drugs is that they can be addictive. GHB and Rohypnol are known to create a physical dependence in users. Rohypnol users have been known to succumb to seizures if they stop taking the drug. GHB is considered to be very difficult to quit; a sudden withdrawal from the drug may produce anxiety, insomnia, tremors, and sweating.

In the case of MDMA, users eventually build up a tolerance to the drug, meaning that they require larger doses to achieve the same effect. However, larger doses cause unpleasant side effects, so the ecstasy experience stops being pleasant at a certain point. But that does not mean MDMA users go clean after they find themselves getting sick or depressed. In

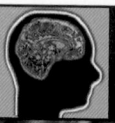 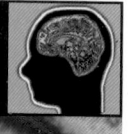

Symptoms of GHB Dependence

In a 1997 issue of the medical journal *Addiction*, researchers at the Haight-Ashbury Free Clinic in San Francisco reported on the addiction trends they saw among GHB users. A typical case, they said, involved a patient they identified as "Ms. A." The researchers reported:

Ms. A described GHB as producing feelings of relaxation, increased libido and marked euphoria. When she abruptly decreased her dose . . . she experienced anxiety that persisted for 1 week. On six subsequent occasions when she discontinued use of GHB she experienced tremor, insomnia and anxiety, which she described as 'feelings of doom.' These symptoms started 12 hours after the last dose of GHB, persisted until she resumed GHB use, and were relieved when she ingested two alcoholic beverages.

Gantt P. Galloway et al, "Gamma-hydroxybutyrate: An Emerging Drug of Abuse that Causes Physical Dependence," *Addiction*, January 1, 1997, p. 91.

many cases, they discard ecstasy and move to other drugs, such as methamphetamine or LSD.

Club drugs also create a psychological dependency in their users. Most users feel as if they need the drug in order to function normally. Psychological dependence can last much longer than physical dependence.

Irreversible Damage

The long-term effects of club drugs have been documented. MDMA is regarded as particularly hazardous because it causes body temperatures to rise. But even in cases where use of the drug does not lead to heatstroke, ecstasy can still cause permanent brain damage. A 1999 study conducted at Johns

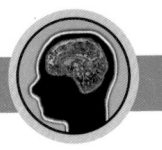

Hopkins University in Baltimore showed that frequent ecstasy users experience memory loss and that the damage is irreversible. Other research suggests that over time ecstasy users may show symptoms of Alzheimer's disease, a condition that mostly afflicts elderly people, slowly destroying their brains and robbing them of their memories. Brain damage caused by ecstasy may also result in symptoms that mimic Parkinson's disease, which causes its sufferers to tremble and lose control of their motor functions.

In another study, the researcher and neurotoxicologist George Ricaurte gave memory tests to people who admitted using ecstasy two weeks before the examinations. During the tests, the ecstasy users did much worse than the "control group"—people who had never taken ecstasy. In addition, computer images of brain scans of ecstasy users showed they had fewer serotonin receptors in their brains than nonusers, which can cause depression. Ricaurte also gave doses of

Dancers on ecstasy risk heatstroke due to the drug's side effects combined with the steamy, crowded conditions typical of most raves.

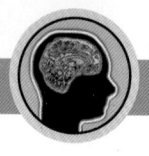

MDMA to lab monkeys. He planned to give ecstasy every three hours to five monkeys, but shortly after starting the experiment one monkey died and another monkey became very sick, so he decided to stop the test.

Alan I. Leshner, a former director of the National Institute on Drug Abuse, has long warned about the long-term effects of club drugs. In an article titled "Club Drugs Aren't 'Fun Drugs,'" Leshner wrote,

> We know that many people report that they've had some memory loss, and now scientific studies have documented that, actually, repeated ecstasy use leads to an interference with normal memory processes, and actually broader thought processes as well.[30]

Depression is another long-term problem of ecstasy use, one that can last for weeks or months after a person stops taking the drug. To cope, some users take more of the drug to cheer themselves up; however, this generally causes a downward spiral into more severe episodes of depression. This is a scenario Olivia Gordon described in her book *The Agony of Ecstasy*. "On the Saturday night I took my first whole e—it lifted me out of my depression for three or four hours—then I came down," she wrote. "I just got more & more freaked out & felt like the walking dead."[31]

Ketamine also causes harmful long-term side effects, including impaired memory and an inability to think clearly. Users of dissociative hallucinogens like ketamine have also developed psychiatric illnesses, including depression and a much more severe form of mental illness known as psychosis, which means the sufferers lose touch with reality. In cases of psychosis, medical treatment is required to enable them to function in society.

Brittney's Story

While people who take club drugs risk heatstroke, kidney failure, memory loss, chronic depression, and other physical

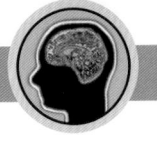

problems, they also risk losing their lives. One teenager who died the first time she tried ecstasy was Brittney Chambers, a high-school student from Superior, Colorado.

On the evening of February 2, 2001, nearly forty of Brittney's friends gathered to help her celebrate her sixteenth birthday. The party was held at the family home, where Brittney's mother, Marcie Chambers, could keep an eye on things. Marcie did not know, however, that Brittney and three of her friends planned to get high on ecstasy during the party. "We wanted to experience this together," Brittney's friend Lisa Weaver told *People*. "I'd heard nothing bad would happen."[32]

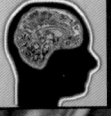 ## Impure Ecstasy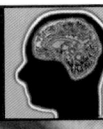

One of the dangers of MDMA is that the pills are manufactured in illegal labs, and may contain toxic additives. *Time* magazine reported that in 1999 at a rave in Oakland, California, attended by some five thousand people, nine had to be transported to the hospital by ambulance. After treating the dancers, doctors concluded that eight of the ravers had ingested something other than MDMA.

Aspirin and caffeine are the most common additives to ecstasy. Underground chemists also add dextromethorphan, or DXM, to the mix. DXM is an ingredient found in over-the-counter cough medicines, but in very large doses it is known to cause hallucinations. A single dose of ecstasy that has been enhanced with DXM often contains as much as thirteen times the amount found in the typical bottle of cough syrup.

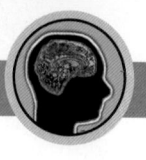

Just after 10 P.M. that night, Brittney swallowed a tablet of ecstasy. About ninety minutes later, the teenager felt sick to her stomach. Brittney and a friend locked themselves in an upstairs bathroom. When Marcie knocked on the bathroom door around midnight, Brittney replied that everything was fine; she and her friend were just talking. Marcie returned about a half-hour later and demanded to be let in. She found her daughter sitting on the floor, surrounded by empty water bottles. Brittney was disoriented. She slurred her words and seemed unable to focus her eyes. "I knew when I saw her eyes that this was drugs,"[33] Marcie said. She went downstairs and called for the paramedics.

MDMA can make its users thirsty, which prompts them to drink large quantities of water—sometimes too much. That is what happened to Brittney. Shortly after taking the pill, Brittney had felt dehydrated and asked for water. She kept drinking water until she started vomiting. She had consumed so much water that her blood became diluted, which reduced the natural salt levels in her body, in turn cutting off the blood supply to her brain. By the time Brittney arrived at the hospital, she was in a coma. Two days later, doctors told Marcie that her daughter's condition was irreversible. Marcie and her husband, Art Ruiz, stood at Brittney's bedside as she was taken off life-support equipment. "We held her hand and told her how much we loved her and that she was going to heaven," Marcie said. "We told her not to be afraid, that she would be with the angels."[38]

The official cause of Brittney's death was water intoxication. A subsequent police investigation resulted in the arrests of six of Brittney's friends. Marcie Chambers told *People*, "I wish I could blame someone, but the truth is Britt made that choice, she took that pill."[35]

Positive Benefits?

Despite the overwhelming evidence that club drugs cause damage to the brain and body, some researchers believe that

MDMA can be an effective treatment for mental illness. When used under controlled circumstances, they claim, severe depression—like that brought on by a rape or other traumatic experience—can be alleviated through doses of MDMA. According to Rick Doblin, a political scientist with a Harvard PhD, ecstasy "can be used in any situation in which people have to confront difficult, emotionally challenging issues, in which avoidance is likely and insight will be helpful."[36]

Doblin said MDMA promotes introspection—users find themselves comfortable with the notion of exploring their own thoughts and coming to terms with what troubles them. For example, Marcela Gomez, a forty-seven-year-old rape victim, told *Newsweek* magazine that for years she suffered from panic attacks caused by the trauma of her rape. She said ecstasy, which she obtained through underground channels, helped her confront her fears. "MDMA lets you open a door and not be traumatized,"[37] she said.

To gain public acceptance of the beneficial qualities of MDMA, Doblin founded the Multidisciplinary Association for Psychedelic Studies (MAPS) and began a campaign to convince the U.S. Food and Drug Administration (FDA) to authorize studies of MDMA involving human test subjects. (In the Johns Hopkins study headed by Ricaurte,

MAPS founder Dr. Rick Doblin claims that MDMA can help people suffering from mental illness.

only lab monkeys were given doses of ecstasy; the human ec-stasy users who participated in the research had consumed MDMA on their own under uncontrolled conditions before the tests were taken.)

After Doblin spent years lobbying the FDA, the agency fi-nally approved a small study at McLean Hospital in Belmont, Massachusetts, which is affiliated with Harvard University's medical school. Under the study, which began in 2005, a dozen patients with incurable cancer were to be given MDMA to determine whether the drug helped alleviate their depression. While the study is small—critics point out that results garnered from twelve patients will not provide con-clusive proof that MDMA can be an effective antidepres-sant—Doblin and other proponents of the drug believe it is only a beginning and more tests should be conducted. Todd Shuster, a physician who treats cancer patients at McLean Hospital, told *Newsweek*, "I thought of MDMA as the rave drug. But the more I read, the more I realized this was a sci-entific question worth asking."[38]

Innocent Victims

The question of whether MDMA can be put to legitimate use may take years, or even decades, to answer. In the mean-time, club drugs remain part of American society, affecting the lives of the people who use them. While those who ingest club drugs may suffer from the side effects, others suffer as well, including the friends and family members who must en-dure the trials of loved ones caught in the cycle of abuse. The victims of club drugs also include innocent teenage girls and young women who unknowingly consume GHB, Rohypnol, and ketamine, making them easy prey for sexual predators.

Chapter 4

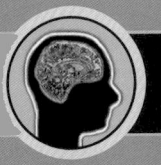

DATE RAPE AND OTHER DANGERS TO SOCIETY

Like those who abuse other illegal narcotics, club drug users are known to engage in other risky behavior—such as driving under the influence, practicing unsafe sex, and taking other addictive and dangerous drugs. But the club drugs GHB and Rohypnol can be involved in situations that have an even more devastating impact: Assailants have been known to slip the drugs into the drinks of teenage girls and young women who, after succumbing to the tranquilizing effects of the drugs, are raped. In recent years, ketamine has also been used in date rape incidents. There is no question, then, that club drugs affect not only the lives of the users but very often affect other people as well.

Radical Shifts in Behavior

People who abuse club drugs eventually admit that their dependency can cause major changes in their lives. Many find themselves doing things they never thought they would do before they began experimenting with drugs, seeking the pleasurable feelings or the loosening of inhibitions that the drugs cause. Ashley, who used ecstasy during high school,

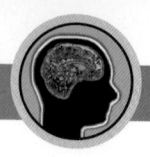

told an interviewer for the PBS documentary *In the Mix* that she often had unprotected sex with boys who got high with her. At one point, she worried whether she could have contracted HIV, the virus that causes the debilitating and often fatal disease AIDS. She said,

> You think about it and you're like, oh my God, I had unprotected sex with this guy, you know. I don't know how many girls he's ever been with, what if I got something. And I was in that situation, I went and I got tested, and HIV tested, and everything, because you can really do things you wouldn't normally do when you were sober and thinking straight.[39]

Meaghan, another teenager interviewed for *In the Mix*, said that ketamine dominated her life so much that she stole to support her habit. She said:

> Just being on K makes you feel like you're drunk, and then being drunk on top of that makes you feel like you're just in another world. It's scary. At one point I was spending $300 a week on drugs. I used to steal money from my parents. I would sell anything I could get my hands on.[40]

Michelle, a former MDMA user, told an interviewer for *In the Mix* how ecstasy came to dominate her life:

> I'd just sit in my room for like, hours. And I wouldn't leave my room until I was ready to get up and go get high again. Basically, I'd just get depressed and get high to cover that up, and it was just a vicious cycle.
>
> I was a cheerleader when I first went to high school. And then my second year I was barely in school.[41]

Driving Under the Influence

Other users get into other kinds of trouble. For example, in 2005 police responded to reports of a woman driving erratically in Tyler, Texas. When police found the suspect, twenty-

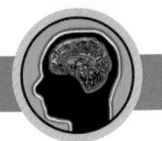

eight-year-old Danielle Lafayette, she was passed out behind the wheel of her car as it idled at an intersection. The officers found her in possession of numerous drugs, including ninety-six tablets of ecstasy, and they took her into custody. Police also found Lafayette's four-year-old daughter sitting in the car. When Danielle was later brought before a jury, it took

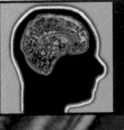 **How Ecstasy Use Leads to Meth**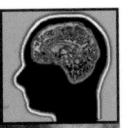

After they have used MDMA for a while, some ravers may look for other ways to get high. One drug they commonly turn to is crystal meth, a highly addictive form of methamphetamine that is smoked in a pipe. Crystal methamphetamine is sometimes considered a club drug because it is often used in nightclubs and at raves.

One reason ecstasy users move on to crystal meth or other drugs is that they can no longer get the same buzz without taking more pills. Stronger doses of ecstasy tend to make users sick to their stomachs. Another reason is the price—a hit of crystal meth is generally about half the cost of a dose of ecstasy.

Like ecstasy, crystal methamphetamine enables users to stay up for long periods of time. However, the drug is highly toxic, and can cause permanent physical and mental damage.

Crystal meth is a strong drug sometimes used in conjunction with club drugs.

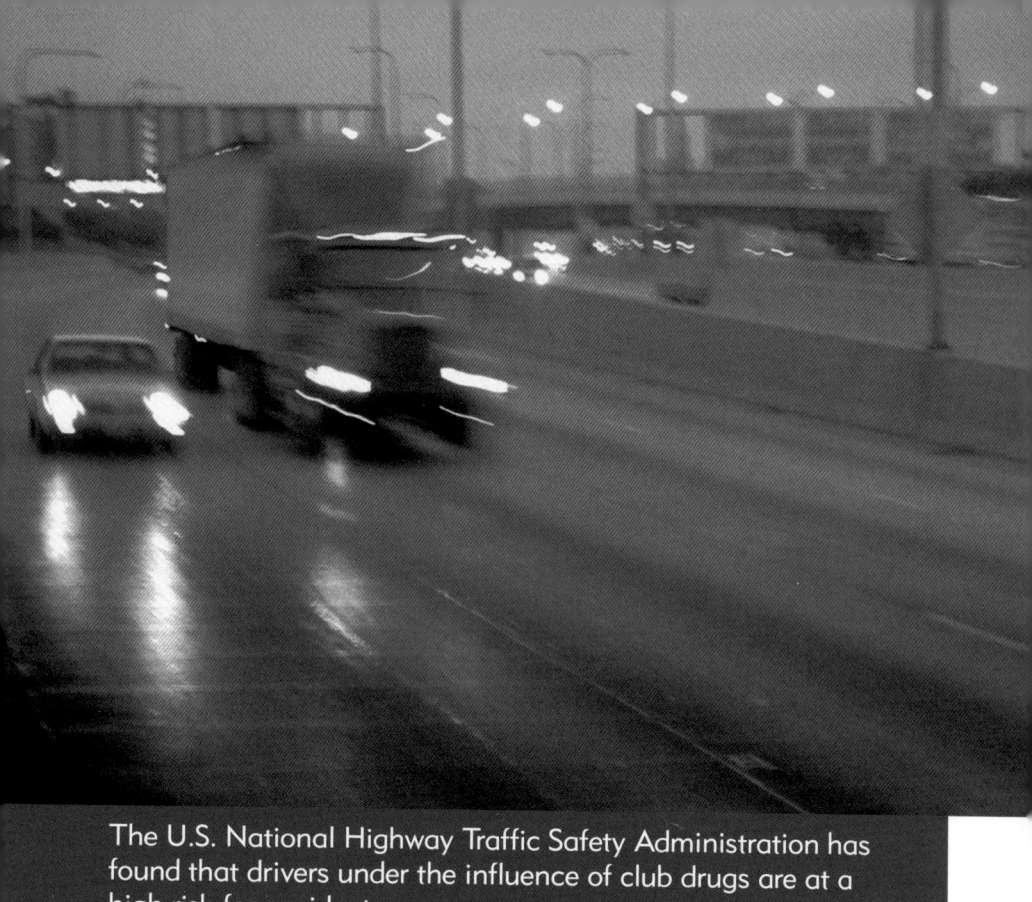

The U.S. National Highway Traffic Safety Administration has found that drivers under the influence of club drugs are at a high risk for accidents.

the jury just twenty minutes to convict her of the charge of driving under the influence with a child. She was sentenced to two years in prison.

Lafayette's young daughter was not injured in that incident, but in other cases drivers high on ecstasy have been involved in serious accidents, causing injury and even death. One such case occurred in 2005 when prosecutors in Lincoln, Nebraska, charged twenty-eight-year-old Jeremy L. Forsgren with causing an accident that injured two people, one critically. According to police, Forsgren raced through Lincoln streets at speeds approaching ninety miles an hour, then crashed into another vehicle. Police said Forsgren told them that the accident occurred at the conclusion of an "eight-day bender"[42] during which, he admitted, he had used ecstasy and other drugs.

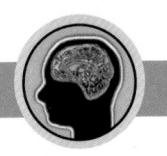

In another such case, in Great Britain, twenty-one-year-old Luke Small was sentenced to six years in prison after crashing his car into another vehicle, killing three people. Small admitted to police that he had smoked marijuana and consumed ecstasy before getting into his car. Before sending Small to jail, Judge Kerry Macgill rebuked him, "Because of your crass stupidity three people died and your family and their families are left devastated."[43]

Sometimes, ecstasy users need not be driving a car to endanger others. Twenty-one-year-old Merlin Spiers was sentenced to nine months in jail after he crashed a forklift in a paper mill, causing a huge roll of paper to fall onto his nineteen-year-old cousin, Rowan Ratcliffe, resulting in fatal injuries to the teenager. Spiers and Ratcliffe had both consumed MDMA before breaking into the paper mill for some mischief. "Fuelled by bravado and Ecstasy an accident was inevitable,"[44] prosecutor Ian Fenny told news reporters at the British Broadcasting Corporation.

Studying the Effects on Drivers

In 2000, the U.S. National Highway Traffic Safety Administration examined issues surrounding drug abuse and driving at a conference in Seattle, Washington. The conference was composed of toxicologists—scientists who study the effects of chemicals and other substances on the human body and human performance. The toxicologists studied sixteen drugs, both legal and illegal, to determine whether people under the influence of those drugs could safely operate motor vehicles. Among the drugs studied were MDMA, GHB, and ketamine.

The toxicologists concluded that users of club drugs should not drive. In their report for the Highway Traffic Safety Administration, the toxicologists wrote:

> [MDMA] can enhance impulsivity and make it difficult for a person to maintain attention during complex tasks. . . . Laboratory studies have demonstrated changes in cognitive, perception and

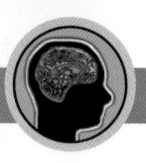

mental associations, instability, uncoordinated gait, and poor memory recall. Distortion of perception, thinking, and memory, impaired tracking ability, disorientation to time and place, and slow reactions are also known performance effects.[45]

Examining the cases of six MDMA users arrested for driving under the influence, the toxicologists found "the subjects were cooperative and laid back, and experienced muscle twitching, body tremors, perspiring, dilated pupils, slow reaction to light, and poor performance on field sobriety tests."[46]

The toxicologists also reviewed arrest records for GHB users. The report on GHB gave details:

The subjects were typically stopped because of erratic driving, such as weaving, ignoring road signs, and near-collisions. Common signs of impairment included confusion and disorientation, incoherent speech, short-term memory loss, dilated pupils, lack of balance and unsteady gait, poor coordination, poor performance of field sobriety tests, copious vomiting, unresponsiveness, somnolence [drowsiness], and loss of consciousness.[47]

As for ketamine, the toxicologists noted that when it is prescribed legally, the drug is meant to put patients to sleep. Their report to the Highway Transportation Safety Board concluded, "The use of ketamine is not conceivably compatible with the skills required for driving."[48]

Club Drugs and Rape

The qualities of GHB and ketamine that make them so dangerous on the highway make them equally dangerous to teenage girls and young women who may consume them at raves or other parties. Finding themselves in a drowsy and dreamy state, women can become victims of rapists. During the past decade, GHB, Rohypnol, and ketamine have all been used as date rape drugs.

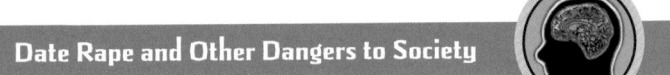

The effects of GHB, Rohypnol, and ketamine can begin within ten minutes of ingestion. The victims lose control of their muscles. Dizziness and sleepiness are common symptoms. The victims may feel the need to lie down. Often, they will fall asleep for ten or twelve hours, then wake up with no memory of what happened. Very often, they have consumed the drugs without knowing it. While a victim is distracted, somebody may slip the drug into her drink. Later, once the drug begins to take effect, the assailant can take advantage of the victim's drugged state to commit a sexual assault.

Some victims recall undergoing out-of-body experiences during the rapes; in such a state, the person feels separated from her body and like an outside observer of what is happening. Victims realize they are being assaulted but find

Date rape incidents involving GHB or Rohypnol became more common during the mid-1990s. Often, the victims would wake up knowing something had happened, but without a clear memory of being assaulted.

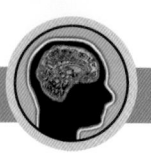

themselves powerless to fend off their attackers. One date rape victim, Jenna, told a writer for *Current Health* magazine that she met a "cool and good-looking guy" named Trevor at a party. After having only two beers, though, Jenna felt dizzy and drunk. When Trevor offered to drive her home, she accepted. At her house, Jenna could hardly stand up and Trevor carried her inside and put her on her bed; the next morning, she woke up sore and saw her clothes piled on the

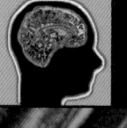 ## The Dangers of BD and GBL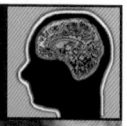

Two drugs that are similar to GHB are 1,4-butanediol, known as BD, and gamma-butyrolactone, which is known as GBL. BD is a chemical used in industrial applications to make polyurethane, which is employed as a finish for furniture; the chemical is also used to make Spandex, the elastic fabric used in athletic garments. At one time, BD could also be found in health food stores, where it was sold as a sleep aid. Because of its industrial uses, BD remains legal, although the U.S. Food and Drug Administration has declared it a health hazard, forbidding its use in products sold for human consumption. As for GBL, before it was made illegal, it was sold as a fat burner and sleep aid. Once in the body, both substances exert the same effects as GHB.

Both BD and GBL remain widely available in the illegal market, and their use as date rape drugs has been chronicled by police. In 2002, a Sioux Falls, South Dakota, man was charged with drugging his child's babysitter with BD before sexually assaulting the girl.

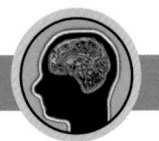

floor. "Oh no," she thought, "he must have raped me! But how can I prove it? I don't remember anything."[49] Her last memory was of Trevor driving her home.

A Crime that Is Hard to Prove

Law enforcement officers are often frustrated in their attempts to track down rapists who give GHB, ketamine, or Rohypnol to unsuspecting women. For starters, date rape victims often do not realize they have been assaulted until well after the act—sometimes days. This means that the physical evidence that can be obtained from their bodies has disappeared or has been washed away. In addition, they often cannot testify in court about the assaults because most victims have no memory of them. Wrote retired New York City police officer John DePresca:

> How about a case where the victim tells you she knows a crime has been committed against her but can't tell you who did it, where it happened, when it happened, how it happened or why it happened? Every investigator will be called to task when looking into a date rape drug. Rapists now have in their lurid arsenal more than a couple of methods to render their victims helpless.[50]

In 2000, Gail Abarbanel, founder and director of the Rape Treatment Center at the Santa Monica–University of California at Los Angeles Medical Center, estimated that as many as 20 percent of rapes in the United States are committed by assailants who employed date rape drugs. She said her center first started noticing the use of the drugs in 1995. "Victims were coming in who believed they had been drugged surreptitiously to incapacitate them for the purpose of sexually assaulting them," she wrote in the *National Institute of Justice Journal.*

Many of these cases followed a similar pattern. Victims were in what seemed like a comfortable social environment, such as a

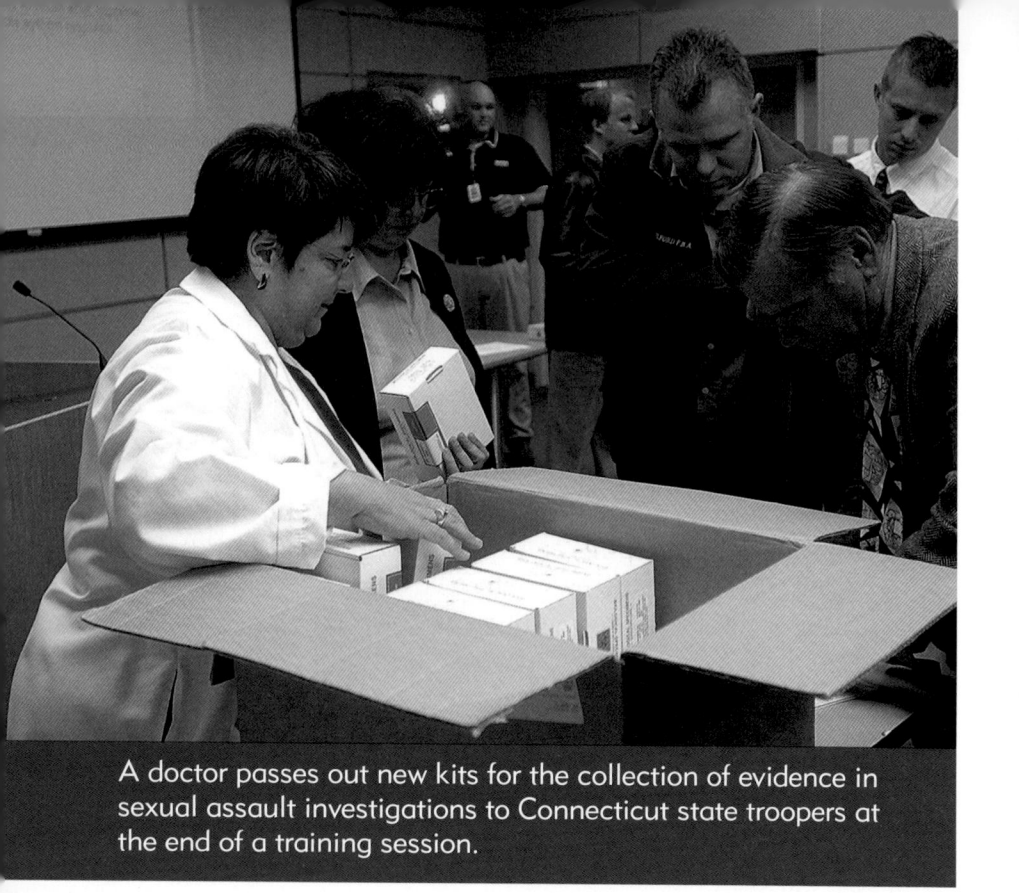

A doctor passes out new kits for the collection of evidence in sexual assault investigations to Connecticut state troopers at the end of a training session.

restaurant, party, or club. Unbeknownst to them, someone slipped a drug into their drink. As they consumed the drink, they began to feel disoriented or sick. The next thing they remembered was waking up hours later, sometimes in a different location.[51]

According to Abarbanel, when victims first reported the assaults, a common reply from police was, "He has his memory, you don't have yours. There's no evidence. The case is closed."[52] In some cases, police were more sympathetic to the plight of the victims and pursued investigations, but without an independent witness—somebody who saw the assailant spike the victim's drink and would be willing to testify—they were often powerless to make an arrest.

Two Key Cases

Women who are secretly slipped the drugs in their drinks face the very real possibility of losing their lives because of the substances as well. That is what happened to teenagers

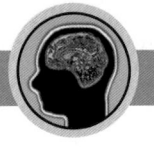

Hillory Janean Farias and Samantha Reid. The deaths of the two girls turned the national spotlight onto date rape drugs.

Hillory, a seventeen-year-old girl from LaPorte, Texas, was a good student and athlete who hoped to win a volleyball scholarship to the University of Texas. In August 1996, just a few weeks before the start of her senior year in high school, she went to a nightclub with some friends. Hillory arrived home at about midnight and told her grandmother she had a headache. She took aspirin and went to bed. The next morning, Hillory's grandmother could not wake her. A police investigation revealed that a soda she had consumed at the nightclub had been spiked with enough GHB to prove fatal.

The tragic 1996 death of Hillory Farias drew greater attention to the problem of date-rape drugs. The photo of Hillory at volleyball camp (she is in the back row, wearing the white tie in her hair) was taken August 4, 1996. That night, she unknowingly ingested a drink spiked with a fatal dose of GHB.

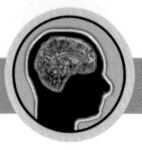

Three years later, fifteen-year-old Samantha "Sammy" Reid of Grosse Isle, Michigan, told her mother she was going to the movies with two girlfriends. Instead of going to the movie theater, though, Sammy and her girlfriends visited an apartment to meet three boys they knew from high school. At the apartment, Sammy and one of her friends accepted an offer of soft drinks. After drinking their sodas, both girls lost consciousness.

After a few hours, the boys took the two girls to the emergency room. Sammy's friend was lucky; she had slipped into a coma but then recovered. Sammy never woke up, however. The teenagers' drinks had been spiked with GHB. "None of the girls ever knew the substance was put in their drinks," Grosse Isle detective John Szczepaniak told a reporter. "Samantha never knew what happened to her."[53] In the Samantha Reid case, the boys who spiked Sammy's drink were convicted on manslaughter charges and sentenced to prison terms of up to fifteen years.

Legal Efforts Intensify

The publicity surrounding the deaths of Hillory Farias and Samantha Reid helped increase awareness of the dangers of GHB, Rohypnol, and other drugs used to facilitate sexual assaults. State and federal lawmakers would soon step in, enacting laws with tough penalties for assailants who employ date rape drugs, while police departments would undergo training to better understand and respond to the threat. Congress and other federal agencies also have taken steps to curtail the illegal manufacture and importation of the drugs into the United States.

Chapter 5

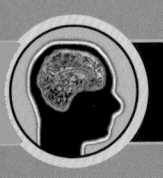

FIGHTING BACK AGAINST CLUB DRUGS

Laws written to protect women from date rapes were only the start of the fight against club drugs. Other laws have increased the penalties for those who sell or use ecstasy, ketamine, GHB, and Rohypnol. Meanwhile, law enforcement authorities have targeted club drugs with the same vigor and resources normally associated with some of the better-known narcotics, such as crystal methamphetamine and cocaine.

Tough New Laws

Congress took the first action against date rape drugs in 1996 when it passed the U.S. Drug-Induced Rape Prevention and Punishment Act. This law was aimed at policing the use of Rohypnol as a date rape drug; it established prison terms of up to twenty years for people who employed Rohypnol in the act of a sexual assault or any other violent crime. Under the act, simply possessing Rohypnol could mean a jail sentence of up to three years.

Four years later, the deaths of Hillory Farias and Samantha Reid prompted Congress to pass a second law making it illegal to manufacture, distribute, or possess GHB. Adopted in

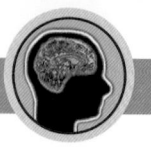

2000, the Hillory J. Farias and Samantha Reid Date-Rape Drug Prohibition Act made the penalty for possessing GHB up to twenty years in prison. The act also made possession of ketamine without a prescription illegal. In addition, the act requires the Department of Health and Human Services to track cases of date rape in which drugs have been employed and submit to Congress annual reports summarizing the threat of date rape drugs in American society.

The federal agency also was required to develop a campaign to educate women as well as law enforcement professionals, teachers, hospital emergency room workers, and others about the symptoms and dangers of date rape drugs. It can be extremely difficult to make arrests in date rape cases, so educating women on preventing and responding to situations properly is important. In many cases, all the investigators have is the physical evidence left on the victim. Without

In 2000, these four men were sentenced to prison for the drug-poisoning death of Samantha Reid. A federal law passed that year mandates longer jail terms for crimes involving GHB or other date-rape drugs.

that, arrests are unlikely, and the extended prison sentences mandated by the tougher legislation are pointless.

Hillory's uncle, Raul Farias, testified before the U.S. House Judiciary Committee when the panel considered the date rape drug law. He told members of the committee:

> Hillory never drank alcohol, never smoked, and was drug free. The investigation has proved all of this, and. . . the one thing that stood out in the investigation, is that Hillory's character was recognized by all that were interviewed. We already knew Hillory was special, but to hear from hundreds of other people, it was just something very special and something very meaningful to the family. . . .
>
> Please put this bill into action. We need to protect our youth; need to protect our daughters, sons, nieces and nephews, and hold people accountable for their actions, especially when it comes to defenseless rape and murder.[54]

Other laws have also been enacted, making it illegal to distribute, as well as abuse, all four major club drugs and their analogs, the drugs that are similar to them. In 2002 Congress adopted legislation making it illegal to stage a rave as a means to sell drugs.

Under Gang Control

What has become clear to law enforcement agencies is that the club drug trade has been taken over by drug kingpins who rake in millions of dollars. The potential profit that can be made by dealing club drugs is enormous. According to the 2003 *Illegal Drug Price and Purity Report* published by the DEA, a street dealer can buy drugs from his supplier—an illegal lab or a middleman—for as little as five dollars per tablet, then sell it at two or three times that price.

Prices differ from city to city. In Philadelphia, according to the 2003 DEA report, the minimum price for a tablet of ecstasy is twenty dollars. At a rave in Miami, an MDMA user

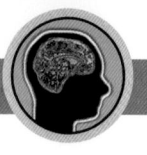
can pay fifteen dollars, while in Dallas, the minimum price for a hit of ecstasy is as little as ten dollars. On the other end of the price range, a raver in New York City might pay as much as thirty-eight dollars for a tablet of MDMA.

Prices for the other club drugs also vary widely. A dose of GHB, which is typically just a fraction of an ounce, can cost from as little as five dollars in Los Angeles to as much as thirty dollars in Atlanta. A dose of ketamine could cost the buyer from as little as three dollars in San Francisco to as much as twenty dollars in Newark.

The illegal labs that create the drugs also make tremendous profits. As noted in the DEA report *Ecstasy and Predatory Drugs*, it can cost as little as fifty cents to produce one tablet of ecstasy. According to the report:

> A typical clandestine laboratory is capable of producing 20–30 kilograms of Ecstasy per day, with one kilogram of Ecstasy producing approximately 7,000 tablets. . . . Although estimates vary, the cost of producing one Ecstasy tablet is between $.50–$1.00. . . . Once the Ecstasy reaches the United States, a domestic cell distributor will charge from $6 to $12 per tablet. The Ecstasy retailer, in turn, will distribute the Ecstasy for $20 to $30 per tablet. At $20 per tablet, one kilogram of Ecstasy would generate $140,000. At $30 per tablet—$210,000.[55]

The Threat of Organized Crime

Because of the demand for club drugs, the business has grown from small-time production in homes into an international multibillion-dollar operation controlled by notorious gangs, many of them headquartered in foreign countries. It is believed that some 70 percent of the ecstasy peddled in the United States is manufactured in illegal laboratories in just two countries—Belgium and the Netherlands.

To combat the importation of ecstasy into the United States, federal drug agents have established working relationships with Dutch and Belgian police. Those efforts appear to

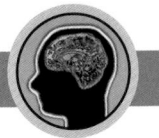

be paying off. According to the DEA, after ecstasy imports were reported in quantities of several million doses in 2000 and 2001, the number of imported doses was cut to fewer than a million by 2003.

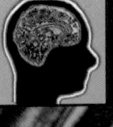 # Drugs and the Russian Mob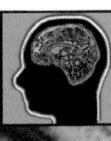

After the Soviet Union broke up in 1991, Russian racketeers began to exploit the country's newly opened society, establishing criminal networks that soon overwhelmed the efforts of Russian police. Today, Russian organized crime figures have become big players in the ecstasy trade in the United States. A report by the U.S. Drug Enforcement Administration calls the Russian Mob "major suppliers of steroids and Ecstasy."

The DEA is also concerned about a gang of ethnically Russian émigrés headquartered in Israel. A 2002 DEA report titled *Russian Organized Crime Groups* discusses the growing role of these groups:

Israeli and Russian Ecstasy trafficking organizations are among the main suppliers of Ecstasy in the United States at this time. According to the Israeli National Police, Israeli and Russian traffickers are typically in their mid-20s, making them younger than most violators associated with criminal groups. These individuals are well educated, extremely mobile, and multilingual. These organizations are involved in the transport of Ecstasy from the Netherlands and Belgium to the United States.

Brazilian police found ecstasy tablets, as well as the chemicals needed to produce the drug, when they raided this illegal lab. Club drugs are often produced outside the United States, then smuggled into the country.

Still, the U.S. State Department is not completely satisfied with actions foreign governments have taken to reduce illegal MDMA exports. The state department has been particularly critical of efforts by law enforcement agencies in the Netherlands to find and shut down illegal labs that manufacture ecstasy and other drugs. The Netherlands has a policy of tolerance toward use of some "soft" drugs—for example, it is legal to possess small amounts of marijuana for personal use. In their reports on the drug war, state department officials have indicated a belief that this attitude of tolerance may contribute to a less-zealous prosecution of the war against drugs. A 2005 report by the State Department's Bureau of European and Eurasian Affairs said, "U.S. law enforcement information indicates the Netherlands still is by far the most significant source country for Ecstasy in the U.S."[56]

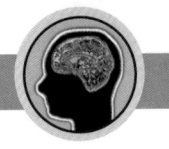

In 2004, proof of the international scope of the illegal ecstasy trade surfaced at Johannesburg International Airport in South Africa, where police seized some three hundred thousand ecstasy tablets believed to carry a street value of nearly $100 million. The drugs arrived aboard a flight that had originated in the Netherlands.

With such large amounts of ecstasy and other club drugs pouring into the United States, use of the drug has spread far beyond raves. *Pulse Check*, a report published in 2004 by the White House Office of National Drug Control Policy, traced the availability of club drugs in most U.S. cities. The *Pulse Check* report found:

> The ecstasy market continues to expand beyond the club scene. For example, in St. Louis and Seattle, it is reported as more mainstream and in the suburbs. In Washington, DC, open-air markets and street sales of ecstasy have emerged. In Atlanta, ecstasy sales have emerged in the city proper. . . .
>
> Ecstasy seller characteristics remain relatively stable, with changes in a few cities. Sellers in Miami are becoming less open than they were in the past, "learning how to avoid law enforcement." Sales have increased in the Black community in Washington, DC. Asian gangs new to Los Angeles are rapidly taking over the ecstasy market. While Atlanta's ecstasy market is generally controlled by overseas groups, the number of local independent sellers is increasing.[61]

Becoming More Dangerous

Law enforcement officials have had some success in cracking down on ecstasy rings in the United States. Major busts include a raid on a New York City apartment where police seized ecstasy pills with an estimated street value of $40 million. The two men who were arrested, David Roash and Israel Ashkenazi—both Israeli citizens—were said to be able to supply their customers with one hundred thousand pills at a time. On the West Coast, after successfully carrying out an

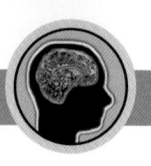

operation known as "Green Clover," local police and federal agents announced they had broken a major ecstasy ring. They arrested thirty people in California and Colorado, including the drug dealer who allegedly supplied ecstasy to the party where Brittney Chambers consumed a fatal dose. In making the bust in 2001, police in California and Colorado seized some eighty-five thousand doses of MDMA.

However, as the club drug trade grows more lucrative, it also becomes more dangerous for police officers tasked with shutting down drug rings. Dealers routinely arm themselves for protection. Mark Kleiman, a professor of public policy at the University of California at Los Angeles, told *Washington Monthly* magazine, "A street market for any expensive drug is going to be enormously disruptive to the community. This is where MDMA can get scary."[58]

Tom Lowe, the lead ecstasy investigator for the Pennsylvania attorney general's office, told *Washington Monthly* that his job used to require him to work undercover at raves, where he would blend in with the crowd and look for MDMA dealers to bust. Most of the dealers he arrested were young people from comfortable suburban homes who were naive about the tactics police were using. As a result, Lowe simply approached an ecstasy dealer, offered to buy a tablet, and, when money changed hands, he made the arrest. But a recent investigation took him into a tough neighborhood of York, Pennsylvania, where he closed down an ecstasy ring operated by armed members of the Latin Kings gang. "It's a whole new ballgame," Lowe told the magazine. "It's not just white suburban ravers anymore."[59]

Targeting the Drugs and the Raves

While the enormous potential profits may inspire those who manufacture and sell ecstasy and other club drugs, they take enormous risks when they go into the business. If they are caught selling club drugs in the United States, the penalties can be quite severe.

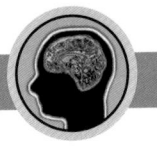

In 1970, Congress passed the U.S. Controlled Substances Act, designating five "schedules" under which all drugs are classified. Schedule I drugs are considered the most dangerous—they have the greatest potential for abuse and have no

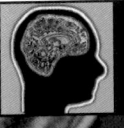 ## Symbols on Ecstasy Pills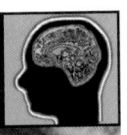

Illegal labs that make ecstasy pills often imprint symbols on the tablets. The DEA has confiscated tablets of ecstasy imprinted with shamrocks, Buddhas, and other images. Sometimes, the ecstasy makers will use a popular logo from American culture. The 2003 DEA report *Ecstasy and Predatory Drugs* warned,

> Marketers create pills often in fluorescent colors and stamped with an appealing image like butterflies, smiley faces, or peace symbols or designer logos like McDonald's or Calvin Klein. This is meant to build brand loyalty, instill confidence, and most of all perpetuate the myth that its use is legitimate and safe.

Ecstasy tablets often feature well-known symbols or logos. From left: the Calvin Klein logo, a peace sign, and the symbol for the euro.

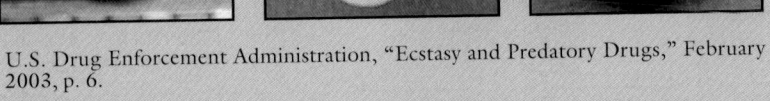

U.S. Drug Enforcement Administration, "Ecstasy and Predatory Drugs," February 2003, p. 6.

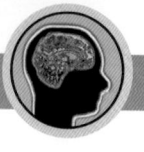

legitimate medical purpose for the treatment of patients. Illegal distributors of Schedule I drugs face the stiffest criminal penalties. Those found guilty of dealing Schedule I drugs face heavy penalties, depending on the amount of drugs involved and the past criminal record of the drug dealer. On the other end of the spectrum are the Schedule V drugs, which are least likely to be abused and are commonly used for legitimate medical purposes.

Ecstasy, which was designated a Schedule I drug in 1985, was specifically targeted by lawmakers in 2000. In that year, Congress adopted the Ecstasy Anti-Proliferation Act, which increased penalties for selling the drug. The act raised the minimum sentence for dealing eight hundred tablets or more of ecstasy from fifteen months to five years in jail. For selling eight thousand pills or more, the sentence was raised to ten years.

SCHEDULE OF CONTROLLED SUBSTANCES

Rating	Examples		Characteristics
Schedule I	· Heroin · LSD · Marijuana · GHB · Psilocybin (mushrooms)	· Mescaline · MDMA (Ecstasy) · PCP · Methaqualone	High potential for abuse; no currently accepted medical use in the United States.
Schedule II	· Opium and Opiates · Methamphetamines · Demerol · Percodan · Cocaine · Amphetamines · Oxycodone · Hydrocodone		High potential for abuse; currently accepted medical use with severe restrictions.
Schedule III	· Anabolic steroids · Codeine · Certain barbiturates · Ketamine (Special K)		Potential for abuse, but less than Schedule I and II substances; currently accepted medical use.
Schedule IV	· Certain barbiturates · Benzodiazepines (Sleeping pills) · Rohypnol		Less potential for abuse; available by prescription.
Schedule V	· Cold and cough medicines		Least potential for abuse; available over the counter.

DEA director Asa Hutchinson discusses the breakup of an ecstasy trafficking ring operating in the south during 2002.

As for the other club drugs, GHB was designated a Schedule I drug in 2000, making the minimum sentences for distributing the drug similar to the sentences for distributing ecstasy. Ketamine, however, continues to have a legitimate medical purpose, so it has been designated a Schedule III drug. Penalties for illegally trafficking ketamine range from five to ten years in prison. The fourth main club drug, Rohypnol, is a Schedule IV drug. Although illegal in the United States, elsewhere it is seen to have legitimate medical value. Trafficking in Rohypnol carries sentences from three to six years in prison. However, because Rohypnol is targeted by the date rape drug laws, making use of the drug in a sexual assault is punishable with twenty years in prison. Of course, aside from federal regulations, there are state laws in place to combat trafficking in narcotics as well. As a result, if drug dealers are prosecuted in local courts instead of federal courts, they still can face many years in prison.

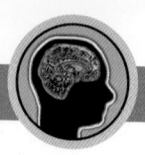
The latest piece of legislation that Congress has enacted against club drugs is the Illicit Drug Anti-Proliferation Act, which it passed in 2003. The law makes it illegal for nightclub owners and rave promoters to allow their properties to be used to promote drug use. The act is based on a similar law adopted in 1986 that made it illegal for the owners of tenements and similar properties to permit their properties to be used as "crack houses," which are places where drug addicts congregate to smoke crack cocaine.

The legislation, called the "Rave Act," applies to property owners who knowingly or intentionally allow drug dealing and drug use to occur during parties, raves, concerts, or similar events on their property. The law established civil penalties for violators, meaning that if they are charged and convicted they do not face prison time. However, a judge can order violators of the Rave Act to pay fines as high as two hundred and fifty thousand dollars.

A police officer outside a nightclub holds a bag containing ketamine. The 2003 Rave Act enables authorities to shut down clubs in which drugs are used.

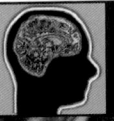 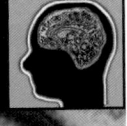
The testimony of Salvatore "Sammy the Bull" Gravano helped send New York mob boss John Gotti to prison for life. Gravano had been a high-ranking mobster, but in 1991, to avoid a lengthy jail sentence, he agreed to tell all he knew about Gotti's criminal organization.

Following the Gotti trial, Gravano served five years in prison for his role in the mob, then entered the federal witness protection program, which provides witnesses in organized crime cases with new identities. Gravano used

the name "Jimmy Moran" and started a new life in Tempe, Arizona. He also went into the ecstasy business. In 2001, Gravano pleaded guilty to heading an operation that distributed some 30,000 ecstasy pills a week in Arizona. Following his guilty plea, Gravano was sentenced to nineteen years in prison.

Former mobster Salvatore "Sammy the Bull" Gravano was sent to prison for operating an ecstasy ring.

Civil liberties groups have protested against the act, claiming it targets a culture rather than a criminal act. These groups argue that there is nothing illegal about rave dancing, techno music, or dancers wearing glow sticks around their necks. Some civil libertarians have likened the Rave Act to racial profiling—the practice whereby police stop and search motorists simply

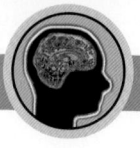

on the basis of the color of their skin and the belief that drug dealers or other criminals are most likely to have certain racial characteristics. In a statement, the Davis, California–based civil liberties group Center for Cognitive Liberty and Ethics, whose board of advisors includes MDMA advocates Alexander Shulgin and Rick Doblin, said:

> Targeting "rave clubs" in an effort to crack down on MDMA use is analogous to targeting anyone with long hair or a tie-died shirt for marijuana possession. Use of such profiling unconstitutionally elevates cultural stereotypes to the level of probable cause. The fact that federal anti-drug agents have to rely on music profiling to enforce anti-MDMA drug laws reveals that the vast majority of people who use MDMA do so responsibly and cannot be identified based on violent or anti-social behavior. Instead, in order to crack down on MDMA use, the police are reduced to employing overbroad policies based on the style of music certain people listen to.[60]

Addicts Must Help Themselves

Lawmakers have enacted legislation outlawing club drugs, and police have used the methods at their disposal to track down and prosecute drug makers and traffickers. But eventually, the drug users themselves must find a way to kick the club drug habit. Shaking an addiction to club drugs often takes months, or even years.

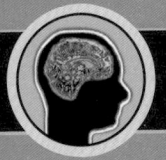

Chapter 6

COMING DOWN
FROM THE HIGH

Club drug users can get help through rehabilitation. Yet because use of these drugs is so widespread, recovering addicts will have to put their party lifestyles behind them to stay drug-free. A former club drug user named James told an interviewer for the PBS documentary *In the Mix* that rehab is "more along the lines of finding out who you are, not the 'stoned' you. If you just be yourself a lot more people will want to be around you, and you'll have a much better time with the people you want to be around."[61]

Admitting the Problem

The first challenge for club drug users is to admit to themselves that they are addicted. In many cases, that realization does not occur until after users become physically sick from the side effects of the drugs, find themselves in the throes of depression, or are convinced by friends or family members that they are addicted and need help.

In 2002, former ecstasy user Lynn Marie Smith, author of the book *Rolling Away: My Agony with Ecstasy*, told a subcommittee of the U.S. House Government Reform

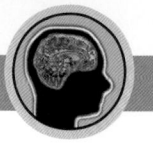

I was placed in a rehabilitation program. During the month-long rehab, I learned how badly I had been hurting myself. With therapy, I decided that you don't have to prove who you are to anyone but yourself. . . .

I have lost all the friends who used to get high with me. But were they really my friends? Staying friends with them would be detrimental to my recovery. . . .

The hardest part is admitting that you have a problem and that you need help. Once you get past that, you are on the right path. As for me, I feel like I gained my childhood back.[64]

Before leaving rehabilitation, most people are urged to make new friends and take part in organized activities. If they are still in school, they are encouraged to participate in sports or other school organizations where their performance can be monitored and drug use is prohibited. If they are old enough, they are urged to find new places to live in new

Some chronic users of club drugs must enter inpatient rehabilitation programs to kick their dependence on the drugs.

The Center For Drug-Free Living

FLORIDA DEPARTMENT OF CHILDREN & FAMILIES

carf

United Way

712

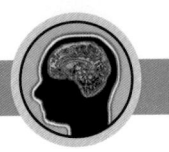

neighborhoods and to start new jobs where they do not come in contact with old friends or old habits.

Rehabilitation is a difficult experience for everyone, but ecstasy users face an additional obstacle to recovery. Specifically, because MDMA increases feelings of depression, former ecstasy users must fight this mental illness as well. The problems associated with this drug last long after the rehab program ends. It may take the former ecstasy users months, or even years, before they can be free of depression.

Fighting Against Depression

In *The Agony of Ecstasy*, Olivia Gordon described how ecstasy caused her to fall into a deep depression and experience unease, anxiety, terror, and panic attacks. Eventually, she was diagnosed with psychotic and personality disorders. She wrote,

> The depression was physiological. For the first days I had thought it was a physical ailment, so forceful was the panic in my heart. Yet I realized instinctively that I had actually entered another realm of sensation, some no-man's land between the physical and the mental. I seemed to be enclosed within a film of pain that I felt in my heart and my head and saw all around me yet which also seemed to be in its own bubble outside the universe. My way of breathing changed. For the first time in my life, I could no longer sleep unless the window was open. My short-breathedness and claustrophobia while panicking were recalled by any airless space. I was afraid also of breathing too deeply, since that was what people did on ecstasy, which reminded me of my panic attacks when rushing on e. This was unfortunate, since all the anti-anxiety self-help books I found recommended deep breathing. What would cure anyone else from depression was the one thing that would make me worse. It seemed that the relaxation of deep breathing could go too far and turn to panic.[65]

To fight depression, most recovering ecstasy users must undergo psychiatric counseling. In many cases, they are pre-

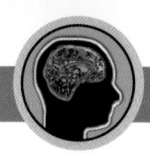

scribed antidepressant drugs, such as Prozac, to help them regain their mental health, but that may not be enough. According to Lynn Marie Smith, her depression was so strong that she was confined to a psychiatric ward for two weeks. "The first few days I refused to take medications because I was so paranoid and I was afraid that I was swallowing more Ecstasy," she said. "I never thought this drug could do this to me."[66]

Prevention Through Education

MDMA and the other club drugs are included in antidrug programs sponsored by national groups such as the Partnership for a Drug-Free America. In 2002, for example, the Partnership launched a national advertising campaign warning about the dangers of ecstasy. According to Steve Pasierb, president and CEO of the Partnership, the group's research showed "widespread false information about Ecstasy as a low-risk, great-high experience, and that misinformation led to very weak attitudes against Ecstasy."[67]

Another national program that focused attention on club drug abuse was Operation X-Out, which was sponsored by the Drug Enforcement Administration. In 2002 and 2003, the DEA organized town meetings in several American communities where solutions to the spread of club drugs were discussed by a wide range of attendees—educators, health experts, students, rape crisis counselors, and citizens.

As for those club drugs that get used as date rape drugs, police and educators feel they have a special duty to help girls and young women understand the dangers of those drugs. As a result, law enforcement officials urge girls never to go to clubs or parties unless accompanied by friends they trust; they advise that friends should watch each other's drinks if they leave for the dance floor or to use the restroom. Also, girls should avoid drinking beverages from common containers, such as punch bowls, unless they are familiar with and comfortable with the person who prepared the punch as well as

the person who is serving it. Women who legally can drink should be wary of bartenders as well—police have prosecuted bartenders who were paid by rapists to drop doses of GHB or Rohypnol in the drinks of victims.

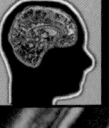 **Parents' Attitudes About Ecstasy**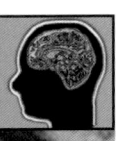

Many parents are unlikely to talk to their children about the dangers of ecstasy, according to a 2003 survey conducted by the Partnership for a Drug-Free America. Of the 1,228 parents surveyed, 92 percent said they were aware of ecstasy, and 90 percent believed the drug to be dangerous. Yet, the Partnership found that just 24 percent of parents advised their children to stay away from ecstasy. "Most parents remain surprisingly unfazed, unmotivated and non-responsive to the threat of Ecstasy in America," according to Steve Pasierb, president and CEO of the Partnership, in a press release announcing the study's results. "The majority of parents have heard about the risks of using this drug, but few are translating that awareness into preventative action at home."

Pasierb suggested that parents may not be comfortable talking about ecstasy with their children because they do not understand the drug themselves. He said parents are much more relaxed talking about more familiar substances, such as marijuana and alcohol. "They don't truly understand what the drug is, or they don't believe their children are at risk," according to Pasierb.

Partnership for a Drug-Free America, "Survey: Majority of Parents Not Responding to Ecstasy Threat," January 6, 2003, p. 1.

Actress Erika Christensen discusses teenage drug use during a program as part of the DEA's Operation X-Out in 2002.

Women who suspect they may have been the victims of date rape drugs are urged to call police as soon as they are capable of dialing the phone. They are told to seek medical attention when they are able. Even though the rape may have occurred hours earlier, when the victim arrives at the hospital medical professionals still may be able to find physical evidence of sexual contact. Victims should not shower before going to the emergency room. They also should not urinate before they are examined, since they may be asked to provide a urine specimen, which can be analyzed for the presence of date rape drugs.

Victims should save the clothes they wore at the time of the assault and turn them over to police because the clothes may include physical evidence. If victims still have the glasses that held their drinks, they should turn them over to police as well. Victims should write down all the details of the at-

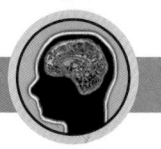

tack that they can remember. All of these things may provide enough evidence for police to piece together a case and bring charges against the assailants.

Trying to Make Raves Safer

Each week, raves continue to draw hundreds, even thousands, of participants. Internet sites are now devoted to announcing times and locations for raves. There are magazines devoted to rave culture, and in recent years Hollywood has created rave-oriented films. Some organizations have also been created with the intent of making raves safer.

These groups, such as California-based DanceSafe, believe that ravers will continue to use drugs. Rather than trying to stop drug use, the groups want to ensure that the ravers take unadulterated drugs. While MDMA and other club drugs are dangerous for many reasons, compounding the danger is the fact that they often are made in unclean environments using industrial chemicals and other harmful products. Also, some illegal manufacturers are known to substitute dangerous look-alike drugs for MDMA. One drug that is commonly sold as ecstasy is in fact paramethoxy-amphetamine, an analog of methamphetamine that is cheap to produce but contains many highly toxic chemicals.

DanceSafe provides volunteer technicians at raves who perform quick chemical analyses on drugs to determine their purity. The group claims its quick tests can usually tell

DanceSafe volunteers test ecstasy for toxic additives during a rave. The volunteers are rarely photographed, because they are handling illegal drugs.

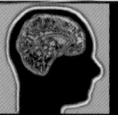

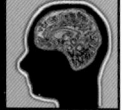

In 1997, Rohypnol manufacturer Hoffman-LaRoche introduced the drug in a new form. The company claimed that its changes would make it harder to use the drug in date-rape assaults. Before the changes, Rohypnol appeared as a white tablet with the word "Roche" stamped on one side (pictured, top). Typically, an assailant would grind up the tablet and drop the powder into a victim's drink.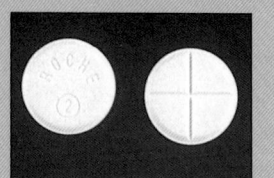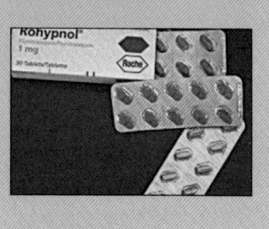

The company changed the color and shape of the tablet, making it green and oblong. It also incorporated a dye that turns a drink blue if the tablet is dropped in it. In addition, the new pill takes longer to dissolve in liquid.

Cynthia R. Knowles, author of the book *Up All Night: A Closer Look at Club Drugs and Rave Culture*, believes that the company did not do enough. Noting that most druggings occur at dimly lit parties and bars, she wrote:

> [These changes are] fine if you are drinking a clear liquid from a clear glass in a well-lit room. The slowed dissolution rate, intended to increase detectability, is also fine if you are sipping your drink through a straw, drawing from the bottom of the glass. Unfortunately, many of us have accidentally swallowed objects [in drinks,] making one wonder how detectable a little sand at the bottom of a glass would actually be.

Cynthia R. Knowles, *Up All Night: A Closer Look at Club Drugs and Rave Culture.* Geneseo, NY: Red House Press, 2001, p. 62.

whether a raver is taking MDMA or another, possibly more dangerous, drug. During the chemical test, a technician will shave off a sliver of the ecstasy pill and immerse it in a drop of solution. If the sample turns black, according to Dance-Safe, it is pure MDMA; if it turns other colors, chances are it has been spiked with dextromethorphan, methamphetamine, or other drugs. Emanuel Sferios, the founder and executive director of DanceSafe, said that at one rave, his organization tested two hundred pills and found forty of them containing dextromethorphan.

Harm Reduction Strategy

DanceSafe claims to have saved many rave dancers from chemical poisonings. Sferios calls DanceSafe's work a "harm reduction" program, and compares DanceSafe's work to needle exchange programs for intravenous drug users, which provide addicts with clean needles in order to prevent the spread of diseases like HIV and hepatitis. He explained:

> [H]arm reduction is an alternative approach to dealing with societal drug use or other criminalized behavior, like prostitution. It works with people to manage their behavior and minimize the harm that might result. Harm reduction provides an alternative to the "abstention only" model. While abstention is the only way to avoid all the harms associated with drug use, many people choose not to abstain. As long as that's the case, regardless of our moral stance on recreational drug use, it presents an immediate need to minimize these harms. Harm reduction programs provide accurate and useful information on drugs, information that drug users can utilize to minimize the risks and the potential harms for their use.[68]

Some police departments have been willing to work with DanceSafe. The DanceSafe technician conducts the test in the open, potentially under the eyes of an undercover drug agent who may be prowling through the rave. In some cities,

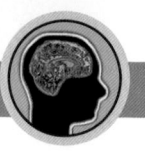

DanceSafe has received agreements from the police not to arrest the dancers who ask for their ecstasy to be tested.

But many law enforcement agencies vehemently oppose the actions of DanceSafe and similar groups. The DEA, for example, warns ravers to be wary of the chemical tests performed at raves, believing they are unreliable. According to a DEA report, "Color testing of drug samples does not assess the amount of the drug in a tablet, nor any contaminant such as strychnine, LSD, or PCP. Tablets often deemed 'safe' by these organizations can, in fact, be deadly."[69] The agency stresses that ecstasy and the other club drugs are highly dangerous narcotics in their own right, regardless of whether they have been tainted with other drugs or toxic substances.

Additionally, the DEA report charges, "Many law enforcement agencies believe that the practices of harm reduction organizations actually encourage drug use, and some have seen a correlation between party drug overdoses and increases in the activities of those organizations."[70]

Continuing Education

The recent results of the *Monitoring the Future* studies, which show club drug use declining, indicate that young people are getting the message that club drugs are habit-forming and dangerous. But judging by the continual popularity of raves, there is no question that the dangers of club drugs still are not fully understood by some young people. In Brittney Chambers' home town of Superior, Colorado, the community responded to the tragedy of her death by raising money for a new youth center where a strong antidrug message is delivered to young people who attend. Similar centers and other organizations continue working every day to educate all citizens about these dangerous substances.

NOTES

Introduction: A New Drug Threat

1. "Overall Teen Drug Use Continues Decline; But Use of Inhalants Rises," University of Michigan news release, December 21, 2004. www.monitoringthefuture.org/pressreleases /04drugpr_complete.pdf.
2. U.S. Senate Caucus on International Narcotics Control, *Statement for the Record by the National Institute on Drug Abuse*, 106th Cong., 2nd sess., July 25, 2000. www.drug-abuse/gov/Testimony/7-25-00Testimony.html.

Chapter 1: Rave Culture and Club Drugs

3. Quoted in Benjamin Wallace-Wells, "The Agony of Ecstasy," *Washington Monthly*, May 1, 2003, p. 14.
4. Cynthia R. Knowles, *Up All Night: A Closer Look at Club Drugs and Rave Culture*. Geneseo, NY: Red House Press, 2001, p. viii.
5. "Raves," National Drug Intelligence Center information bulletin, April 2001. www.usdoj.gov/ndic/pubs/656 /656p.pdf.
6. Eric Nagourney, "The Fight Against Ecstasy," *New York Times Upfront*, December 10, 2001, p. 8.
7. Nagourney, "The Fight Against Ecstasy," p. 8.
8. "Raves," National Drug Intelligence Center information bulletin.
9. Simon Reynolds, *Generation Ecstasy*. New York: Routledge, 1999, p. 85.
10. Reynolds, *Generation Ecstasy*, pp. 84–85.
11. Reynolds, *Generation Ecstasy*, p. 83.
12. Quoted in John Cloud, "Ecstasy: Happiness Is . . . a Pill?" *Time*, June 5, 2000, p. 63.

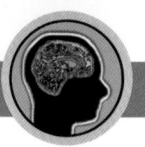

13. G.S. Yacoubian Jr., C. Boyle, C.A. Harding, and E.A. Loftus, "It's a Rave New World: Estimating the Prevalence and Perceived Harm of Ecstasy and Other Club Drug Use Among Club Rave Attendees." http://mdma.net/raves/.
14. Yacoubian, Boyle, Harding, and Loftus, "It's a Rave New World."
15. Jimi Fritz, *Rave Culture: An Insider's Overview*. Victoria, British Columbia: Small Fry Press, 1999, p. 140.
16. Fritz, *Rave Culture: An Insider's Overview*, p. 139.

Chapter 2: The Evolution of Club Drugs

17. Quoted in Julie Holland, ed., *Ecstasy: The Complete Guide*. Rochester, VT: Park Street Press, 2001, p. 12.
18. Quoted in Cloud, "Ecstasy: Happiness Is . . . a Pill?," p. 65.
19. Marsha Rosenbaum and Rick Doblin, "Why MDMA Should Not Have Been Made Illegal," in *Studies in Crime, Law and Justice*, vol. 7. Thousand Oaks, CA: SAGE Publications, 1991. www.psychedlic-library.org/rosenbaum.htm.
20. E.F. Domino, P. Chodoff, and G. Corssen, "Pharmacological Effects of Cl-581," June 18, 1984. www.garfield.library.upenn.edu/ classics1984/A1984SU44500001.pdf.
21. Domino, Chodoff, and Corssen, "Pharmacological Effects of Cl-581."
22. Quoted in Kit Kelly, *The Little Book of Ketamine*. Berkeley, CA: Ronin Publishing, 1999, p. 6.
23. Quoted in Kelly, *The Little Book of Ketamine*, p. 22.
24. John DePresca, "Date Rape Drugs," *Law and Order*, October 1, 2003, p. 210.
25. Clark Staten, "'Roofies,' the New 'Date Rape' Drug of Choice," Emergency Response and Research Institute news release, January 6, 1996. www.emergency.com/roofies.htm.

Chapter 3: The Physical Effects of Club Drugs

26. Larry Smith, "Experts Answer Your Top Questions About Ecstasy," *Teen People*, August 1, 2003, p. 240.

27. U.S. House Subcommittee on Crime, House Judiciary Committee, "Recreational Use of Club Drugs Is Harmful," 106th Cong., 2nd sess., June 15, 2000.

28. Reynolds, *Generation Ecstasy*, p. 85.

29. Holland, *Ecstasy: The Complete Guide*, p. 171.

30. Alan I. Leshner, "Club Drugs Aren't 'Fun Drugs,'" National Institute on Drug Abuse. www.drugabuse.gov/Published_Articles/fundrugs.html.

31. Olivia Gordon, *The Agony of Ecstasy*. London: Continuum, 2004, p. 64

32. Bill Hewitt, Maureen Harrington, and Kate McKenna, "Bitter Pill: One Hit of Ecstasy Killed 16-Year-Old Brittney Chambers Whose Sad Case Fuels a New Antidrug Campaign," *People*, March 4, 2002, p. 52.

33. Hewitt, Harrington, and McKenna, "Bitter Pill," p. 52.

34. Hewitt, Harrington, and McKenna, "Bitter Pill," p. 53.

35. Hewitt, Harrington, and McKenna, "Bitter Pill," p. 53.

36. Gary Greenberg and David Malley, "Dr. X," *Rolling Stone*, April 26, 2001, p. 53.

37. Eve Conant, "Ecstasy: A Possible New Role for a Banned Drug," *Newsweek*, May 2, 2005. www.msnbc.msn.com/id /7613571/site/Newsweek/.

38. Conant, "Ecstasy: A Possible New Role for a Banned Drug."

Chapter 4: Date Rape and Other Dangers to Society

39. Quoted in *In the Mix* (PBS documentary), 2001. www.pbs .org/inthemix/ecstasy_index.html.

40. Quoted in *In the Mix*.

41. Quoted in *In the Mix*.

42. "Charge Filed in High-Speed Crash," *Lincoln Journal-Star*, September 7, 2005. www.journalstar.com/articles/2005 /09/07/local/doc431f8d3a01242947648460.txt.

43. Mark Lavery, "Triple Death Driver Jailed," *Leeds Today*, August 27, 2005. www.leedstoday.net/ViewArticle2.aspx?SectionID=39&ArticleID=1128833.

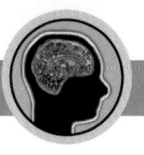

44. Quoted in "Man Sentenced in Cousin's Death," BBC News, September 2, 2005. http://news.bbc.co.uk/2/hi/uk_news/england/devon/4209992.stm.
45. U.S. National Highway Traffic Safety Administration, "Drugs and Human Performance Fact Sheets: Methylenedioxymethamphetamine." www.nhtsa.dot.gov/people/injury/research/job185drugs/methylenedioxymethamphetamine.htm.
46. U.S. National Highway Traffic Safety Administration, "Drugs and Human Performance Fact Sheets: Methylenedioxymethamphetamine."
47. U.S. National Highway Traffic Safety Administration, "Drugs and Human Performance Fact Sheets: Gamma-Hydroxybutyrate." www.nhtsa.dot.gov/people/injury/research/job185drugs/gamma-hydroxybutyrate.htm.
48. U.S. National Highway Traffic Safety Administration, "Drugs and Human Performance Fact Sheets: Ketamine." www.nhtsa.dot.gov/people/injury/research/job185drugs/ketamine.htm.
49. Quoted in Melissa Abramovitz, "The Knockout Punch of Date Rape Drugs," *Current Health*, March 1, 2001, p. 18.
50. DePresca, "Date Rape Drugs," p. 210.
51. Quoted in Gail Abarbanel, "Learning From Victims," *National Institute of Justice Journal*, April 2000, p. 11.
52. Abarbanel, "Learning From Victims," p. 11.
53. Quoted in Peter Vilbig, "New Highs, New Risks," *New York Times Upfront*, May 5, 2000, p. 10.

Chapter 5: Fighting Back Against Club Drugs

54. U.S. House Judiciary Committee, Controlled and Uncontrolled Substances Used to Commit Date Rape: Hearing before the Subcommittee on Crime on H.R. 1530, 105th Cong., 2nd sess., 1998. http://commdocs.house.gov/committees/judiciary/hju62309.000/hju62309_0f.htm.
55. U.S. Drug Enforcement Administration, "Ecstasy and Predatory Drugs," February 2003. www.drugfreeaz.com/PDF/predatory_drugs.pdf.

56. U.S. Department of State Bureau of European and Eurasian Affairs, "Background Note: The Netherlands." www.state.gov/r/pa/ei/bgn/3204.htm.

57. White House Office of National Drug Control Policy, *Pulse Check: Trends in Drug Abuse*, January 2004. www.whitehousedrugpolicy.gov/publications/drugfact/pulsechk/january04/january2004.pdf.

58. Quoted in Wallace-Wells, "The Agony of Ecstasy," p. 8.

59. Quoted in Wallace-Wells, "The Agony of Ecstasy," p. 8.

60. Center for Cognitive Liberty and Ethics, "An Analysis of the Ecstasy Prevention Act of 2001," January 2002. www.cognitiveliberty.org.

Chapter 6: Coming Down from the High

61. Quoted in *In the Mix.*

62. U.S. Drug Enforcement Administration, "Ecstasy and Predatory Drugs."

63. U.S. Drug Enforcement Administration, "Ecstasy and Predatory Drugs."

64. Allegra Miele, "How Getting High Almost Killed Me," *New York Times Upfront*, November 22, 2002.

65. Gordon, *The Agony of Ecstasy*, p. 93.

66. U.S. Drug Enforcement Administration, "Ecstasy and Predatory Drugs."

67. Partnership for a Drug-Free America, "The Hearst Foundation Inc. Awards Grant to Partnership For a Drug-Free America for National Ecstasy Campaign," January 6, 2003. www.drugfree.org/Portal/About/NewsReleases/The_Hearst_Foundation_Inc_Awards_Grant_to_Part/.

68. Quoted in Holland, *Ecstasy: The Complete Guide*, p. 170.

69. U.S. Drug Enforcement Administration, "Ecstasy and Predatory Drugs."

70. U.S. Drug Enforcement Administration, "Ecstasy and Predatory Drugs."

ORGANIZATIONS TO CONTACT

DanceSafe
536 45th St.
Oakland, CA 94609
(510) 834-7500
www.dancesafe.org

DanceSafe provides volunteer technicians who test ecstasy at raves and similar events to determine the drug's purity level. The organization maintains fifteen chapters and affiliated groups in American and Canadian cities.

Drug Enforcement Administration
Mailstop: AXS
2401 Jefferson Davis Highway
Alexandria, VA 22301
(202) 307-1000
www.usdoj.gov/dea

The U.S. Justice Department's chief antidrug law enforcement agency is charged with investigating the illegal narcotics trade in the United States and helping local police agencies with their antidrug efforts. The agency maintains 237 field offices in the United States and offices in more than fifty foreign countries.

Multidisciplinary Association for Psychedelic Studies
2105 Robinson Avenue
Sarasota, FL 34232
(941) 924-6277
www.maps.org

Founded in 1986 by Harvard University-educated political scientist Rick Doblin, MAPS sponsors scientific research into the use

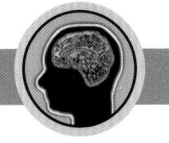

of MDMA as an antidepressant and lobbies Congress and federal agencies to loosen restrictions on the use of the drug.

Narcotics Anonymous
PO Box 9999
Van Nuys, CA 91409
(818) 773-9999
www.na.org

Established in the 1950s, Narcotics Anonymous supports more than twenty thousand groups in the United States and some one hundred foreign countries. Their weekly meetings serve as forums for members to help one another emerge from their addictions.

National Drug Intelligence Center
319 Washington Street, 5th Floor
Johnstown, PA 15901-1622
(814) 532-4601
www.usdoj.gov/ndic

Part of the U.S. Justice Department, the center provides intelligence on drug trends to government leaders and law enforcement agencies. Each year, the center produces the National Drug Threat Assessment, which includes information on the spread of club drugs in the United States.

National Institute on Drug Abuse
6001 Executive Boulevard, Room 5213
Bethesda, MD 20892-9561
(301) 443-1124
www.nida.nih.gov

Part of the National Institutes of Health, the NIDA's mission is to help finance scientific research projects that study addiction trends and treatment of chronic drug users.

Partnership for a Drug-Free America
405 Lexington Avenue, Suite 1601
New York, NY 10174

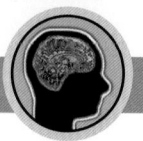

(212) 922-1560.
www.drugfreeamerica.org

Funded by American corporations, media organizations, health professionals, and educators, the Partnership helps convince young people to stay away from drugs.

White House Office of National Drug Control Policy
Drug Policy Information Clearinghouse
PO Box 6000
Rockville, MD 20849-6000
(800) 666-3332
www.whitehousedrugpolicy.gov

The White House Office of National Drug Control Policy was established to develop a national strategy to combat illegal drug use. The office acts as a liaison serving the different federal drug investigation and research agencies. It helps provide information to state and local agencies that fight drug abuse.

FOR FURTHER READING

Books

Anne Alvergue, *Ecstasy: The Danger of False Euphoria*. New York: Rosen Publishing Group, 1998. Basic overview of MDMA use, including stories of teen users who come to terms with their addictions.

Kristine Brennan, *Ecstasy and Other Designer Drugs*. New York: Chelsea House Publishers, 2000. Overview of club drug use in American society; includes a number of contacts for young people who need help fighting their addictions.

Jay Bridges, *Everything You Need to Know About Having an Addictive Personality*. New York: Rosen Publishing Group, 1998. Defines addiction and offers tips on how to avoid getting hooked on drugs, alcohol, gambling, and junk food. For teens who already face addiction, the book recommends techniques and resources they might find helpful in kicking their habits.

Margaret O. Hyde and John F. Setaro, *Drugs 101: An Overview for Teens*. Brookfield, CT: Twenty-first Century Books, 2003. Covers the abuse of several drugs. Provides readers with information on the health effects of drug abuse and includes a chapter on club drugs with a summary of the Hillory Farias case.

Pierre Mezinsky, Melissa Daly, and Francoise Jaud, *Drugs Explained: The Real Deal on Alcohol, Pot, Ecstasy and More*. New York: Harry N. Abrams, 2004. Overview of many addictive substances, including MDMA. Includes a diary by 13-year-old "Emily," who writes about how her friends fall into drug and alcohol abuse.

Lynn Marie Smith, *Rolling Away: My Agony with Ecstasy*. New York: Atria Books, 2005. Smith tells her story of addiction and

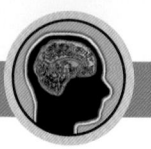

recovery and includes examples of her poetry written both while she was immersed in the rave scene and afterwards as she struggled through drug rehabilitation.

Solomon H. Snyder, ed., *Drugs and the Brain*. New York: Chelsea House, 1987. The book concentrates on how many drugs, including MDMA, affect neurotransmitters and brain cells.

Martin Torgoff, *Can't Find My Way Home: America in the Great Stoned Age, 1945-2000*. New York: Simon and Schuster, 2004. A comprehensive history of illegal drug use in America, covering the hippies of the 1960s, disco clubs of the 1970s, and the rave scene in the 1990s.

WORKS CONSULTED

Books

Jimi Fritz, *Rave Culture: An Insider's Overview*. Victoria, British Columbia: Small Fry Press, 1999. A rave culture insider writes about the music, parties, and drugs and includes personal stories from dozens of dancers and deejays.

Olivia Gordon, *The Agony of Ecstasy*. London: Continuum, 2004. The teenage author of this book tells how she found herself caught up in rave culture, addicted to ecstasy, and battling depression.

Julie Holland, ed., *Ecstasy: The Complete Guide*. Rochester, VT: Park Street Press, 2001. Thorough examination of MDMA, giving voice to physicians and others who warn of the drug's effects as well as mental health professionals who suggest the drug could be an effective antidepressant.

Kit Kelly, *The Little Book of Ketamine*. Berkeley, CA: Ronin Publishing, 1999. Charts the growth and popularity of the drug from its creation as a painkiller to its discovery by New Age drug gurus and use in the rave scene.

Cynthia R. Knowles, *Up All Night: A Closer Look at Club Drugs and Rave Culture*. Geneseo, NY: Red House Press, 2001. Examines the drugs that have become widespread in rave culture and documents efforts by legislators to outlaw club drugs.

Simon Reynolds, *Generation Ecstasy*. New York: Routledge, 1999. Coast-to-coast look at the rave scene in America. Includes a history of MDMA, covering how the drug came to dominate rave culture.

Periodicals

Gail Abarbanel, "Learning From Victims," *National Institute of Justice Journal*, April 2000.

Melissa Abramovitz, "The Knockout Punch of Date Rape Drugs," *Current Health*, March 1, 2001.

Karen Breslau, Ashley Fantz, and Kevin Peraino, "The 'Sextasy' Craze," *Newsweek*, June 3, 2002.

John Cloud, "Ecstasy/Happiness Is . . .a Pill?" *Time*, June 5, 2000.

John DePresca, "Date Rape Drugs," *Law and Order*, October 1, 2003.

Gantt Galloway, S.L. Frederick, Frank E. Staggers Jr., and Marco Gonzales, "Gamma-hydroxybutyrate: An Emerging Drug of Abuse that Causes Physical Dependence," *Addiction*, January 1, 1997.

Gary Greenberg and David Malley, "Dr. X," *Rolling Stone*, April 26, 2001.

Bill Hewitt, Maureen Harrington, and Kate McKenna, "Bitter Pill: One Hit of Ecstasy Killed 16-Year-Old Brittney Chambers Whose Sad Case Fuels a New Antidrug Campaign," *People*, March 4, 2002.

David M. McDowell, "Recreational Use of Club Drugs Is Harmful," testimony given before the U.S. House Subcommittee on Crime, House Judiciary Committee, June 15, 2000.

Allegra Miele, "How Getting High Almost Killed Me," *New York Times Upfront*, November 22, 2002.

Eric Nagourney, "The Fight Against Ecstasy," *New York Times Upfront*, December 10, 2001.

Ellen S. Rome, "It's a Rave New World: Rave Culture and Illicit Drug Use in the Young," *Cleveland Clinic Journal of Medicine*, June 2001.

Science World, "The Agony of Ecstasy," February 26, 2001.

Larry Smith, "Experts Answer Your Top Questions About Ecstasy," *Teen People*, August 1, 2003.

Peter Vilbig, "New Highs, New Risks," *New York Times Upfront*, May 5, 2000.

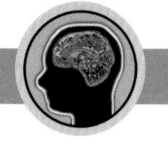

Benjamin Wallace-Wells, "The Agony of Ecstasy," *Washington Monthly*, May 1, 2003.

Shirley Wang, "Radical Relief," *Philadelphia Inquirer*, August 22, 2005.

Internet Sources

BBC News, "Man Sentenced in Cousin's Death," September 2, 2005. http://news.bbc.co.uk/2/hi/uk_news/england /devon/4209992.stm.

CBC News Online, "Is There a Connection Between Crystal Meth and Ecstasy?" August 26, 2004. www.cbc.ca/news /background/drugs/crystalmeth.html.

Eve Conant, "Ecstasy: A Possible New Role for a Banned Drug," *Newsweek*, May 2, 2005. www.msnbc.msn.com/id/761 3571/site/Newsweek/.

E.F. Domino, P. Chodoff, and G. Corssen, "Pharmacological Effects of Cl-581." www.garfield.library.upenn.edu/classics1984/A1984SU44500001.pdf.

Executive Office of the President. White House Office of National Drug Control Policy, *Pulse Check: National Trends in Drug Abuse*, January 2004. www.whitehousedrugpolicy.gov/publications/drugfact/pulsechk/january04/.

———, *Pulse Check: Trends in Drug Abuse*, January 2004. www.whitehousedrugpolicy.gov/publications/drugfact/pulsechk/january04/january2004.pdf.

Mark Lavery, "Triple Death Driver Jailed," *Leeds Today*, August 27, 2005. www.leedstoday.net/ViewArticle2.aspx?SectionID=39&ArticleID=1128833.

Alan I. Leshner, "Club Drugs Aren't 'Fun Drugs,'" National Institute on Drug Abuse. www.drugabuse.gov/Published_Articles/fundrugs.html.

———, testimony before U.S. Senate Caucus on International Narcotics Control. July 25, 2000. www.drugabuse.gov/Testimony/7-25-00Testimony.html.

Lincoln Journal-Star, "Charge Filed in High-Speed Crash," September 7, 2005. www.journalstar.com/articles/2005 /09/07/local/doc431f8d3a01242947648460.txt.

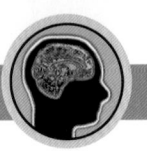

National Drug Intelligence Center, "Raves," April 2001. www.usdoj.gov/ndic/pubs/656/656p.pdf.

National Institute on Drug Abuse, proceedings of the MDMA/Ecstasy Research: Advances, Challenges, Future Directions conference, Ecstasy: What We Know and Don't Know About MDMA, July 2001. http://www.drug abuse.gov/Meetings/MDMA/MDMAExSummary.html

"Officers seize 80,000 Ecstasy pills," Springfield News-Leader, December 2005. http://www.news-leader.com/apps /pbcs.dll/article?AID=/20051220/NEWS01/512200359

Partnership for a Drug-Free America, "The Hearst Foundation Inc. Awards Grant to Partnership For a Drug-Free America for National Ecstasy Campaign," January 6, 2003. www.drugfree.org/Portal/About/NewsReleases /The_Hearst_Foundation_Inc_Awards_Grant_to_Part/.

———, "Survey: Majority of Parents Not Responding to Ecstasy Threat," October 16, 2003. www.drugfree.org/Portal /DrugIssue/Research/PATS Study 2003 - Parents/Sur- vey_-_Majority_of_Parents_Not_Responding_to_Ecs/.

PBS television show, *In the Mix*. www.pbs.org/inthemix/ec- stasy_index.html.

Marsha Rosenbaum and Rick Doblin, "Why MDMA Should Not Have Been Made Illegal," chap. 6 in *Studies in Crime, Law and Justice*. Vol. 7. Thousand Oaks, CA: SAGE Publica- tions, 1991. www.psychedlic-library.org/rosenbaum.htm.

Clark Staten, "'Roofies,' the New 'Date Rape' Drug of Choice," Emergency Response and Research Institute news release, January 6, 1996. www.emergency.com/roofies.htm.

University of Michigan, *Monitoring the Future*, December 2004. www.monitoringthefuture.org.

University of Michigan (news release), "Overall Teen Drug Use Continues Decline; But Use of Inhalants Rises," December 21, 2004. www.monitoringthefuture.org/pressreleases/04 drugpr_complete.pdf.

U.S. Department of Justice, "Ketamine Fast Facts," June 2003. http://www.usdoj.gov/ndic/pubs4/4769/

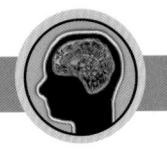

U.S. Department of State Bureau of European and Eurasian Affairs (factsheet). Background Note: The Netherlands. www.state.gov/r/pa/ei/bgn/3204.htm.

U.S. Drug Enforcement Administration, "Drug Intelligence Brief: Russian Organized Crime Groups," January 2002. www.usdoj.gov/dea/pubs/intel/02004/.

U.S. Drug Enforcement Administration, Ecstasy and Predatory Drugs, February 2003. www.drugfreeaz.com/PDF/predatory_drugs.pdf.

U.S. House Judiciary Committee, Controlled and Uncontrolled Substances Used to Commit Date Rape: Hearing before the Subcommittee on Crime on H.R. 1530, 105th Cong., 2nd sess., 1998. http://commdocs.house.gov/committees/judiciary/hju62309.000/hju62309_0f.htm.

U.S. National Highway Traffic Administration, "Drug and Human Performance Fact Sheets: Gamma-Hydroxybutyrate." www.nhtsa.dot.gov/people/injury/research/job 185drugs/gamma-hydroxybutyrate.htm.

U.S. National Highway Traffic Administration, "Drug and Human Performance Fact Sheets: Ketamine." www.nhtsa.dot.gov/people/injury/research/job185drugs /ketamine.htm.

U.S. National Highway Traffic Administration, "Drug and Human Performance Fact Sheets: Methylenedioxymethamphetamine." www.nhtsa.dot.gov/people/injury/research /job185drugs/methylenedioxymethamphetamine.htm.

G.S. Yacoubian Jr., C. Boyle, C.A. Harding, and E.A. Loftus, "It's a Rave New World: Estimating the Prevalence and Perceived Harm of Ecstasy and Other Club Drug Use Among Club Rave Attendees." http://mdma.net/raves/.

Websites

The Drug Library (www.druglibrary.org). This is a comprehensive online library dedicated to providing information about licit and illicit drugs. The library includes medical descriptions of drugs, their histories, dangers, and U.S. laws governing their use.

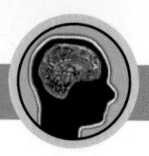

ClubDrugs.org (www.clubdrugs.org). This website, created by the National Institute on Drug Abuse (NIDA), provides information, data on trends, and resources about MDMA (Ecstasy), GHB, Rohypnol, and ketamine.

Drug Facts (www.whitehousedrugpolicy.gov/drugfact/club). This page maintained by the White House Office of National Drug Control Policy provides information about the effects of club drugs.

Ecstasy.org (www.ecstasy.org). This site aims to gather and make accessible objective, up-to-date information about MDMA. It includes links to stories by people who have used ecstasy.

INDEX

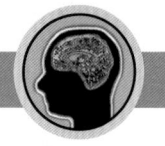

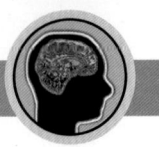

PICTURE CREDITS

ABOUT THE AUTHOR

Hal Marcovitz is a journalist who lives in Chalfont, Pennsylvania with his wife Gail and daughters Michelle and Ashley. He has written more than seventy books for young readers as well as the satirical novel *Painting the White House*.